Letort Paper

NATURAL GAS AS AN INSTRUMENT OF RUSSIAN STATE POWER

Alexander Ghaleb

October 2011

*****

Published by Books Express Publishing
Books Express Publishing, 2011
ISBN 978-1-78039-985-0

Books Express publications are available from all good retail and online booksellers. For
publishing proposals and direct ordering please contact us at: info@books-express.com

*****

Comments pertaining to this report are invited and should be forwarded to: Director, Strategic Studies Institute, U.S. Army War College, 632 Wright Ave, Carlisle, PA 17013-5046.

*****

The author would like to express his gratitude to Professor Nicholas Kenney from the National Defense University for his trenchant critiques and guidance during the research and writing stages of this monograph. I am also grateful to the office of United States Senator Richard Lugar—and particularly to Marik String, Senator Lugar's Professional Staff Member for European and Eurasian Affairs, Committee on Foreign Relations—for encouraging me to examine Russia's use of natural gas as an instrument of coercion.

This monograph was made possible by conversations and interviews with a large number of energy security experts, energy professionals, natural gas lobbyists, and policymakers from both the United States and the European Union. Particular thanks to Alan Hegburg—Senior Energy and National Security Fellow at the Center for Strategic and International Studies—and Rosemary Kelanic—International Security Research Fellow at the Harvard Kennedy School—for helping me to better understand when oil and natural gas can or cannot be used as an instrument of coercion. Also to Vladimir Lefebvre—Senior Fellow at the Center for Advanced Defense Studies—Dr. Jennifer Jefferis—Professor of International Security Studies and Kenneth Baker—Distinguished Professor and Department of Energy Chair at the College of International Security Affairs at the National Defense University—and his research assistant, James Windle, for their early endorsement of my focus on Russian reflexive control.

Furthermore, Robert Cekuta—U.S. Department of State Deputy Assistant Secretary for Energy, Sanctions and Commodities—and Edward Christie—Research Partner with the Pan-European Institute (PEI) of the Turku School of Economics (Finland)—were instrumental in my understanding of the energy security challenges faced by the European Union. I am also grateful to the numerous energy-related lobbying groups—and particularly to the members of the World LP Gas Association for allowing me to attend their WLPGA North America/Europe Summit free of charge—they were very eager to enhance my knowledge with regard to both the advantages and dangers of fossil fuels, and to Dr. Charles Ebinger—Director of the Energy Security Initiative at the Brookings Institution—who taught me a very important lesson about remaining objective when talking to lobbyists.

Finally, I would like to extend my gratitude to a certain senior oil and gas executive from Doha, Qatar, Mark Trgovich—Marketing Director at Qatar International Petroleum Marketing Company—who took precious time away from his incredibly busy schedule to educate me about the geostrategic significance of natural gas in the contemporary security environment; and to all the government agencies and private companies that offered me a job while I was conducting research for this monograph—I hope your offers are still on the table when my military contract expires in January 2014.

*****

FOREWORD

The slow re-emergence of Russia as a world power despite its weak military force is of critical significance for the strategic interests of the United States in Europe. Since the Cold War, Russia has been perceived as a broken nation that no longer represents a threat to the North Atlantic Alliance. This monograph emphasizes that Russia overcame this major vulnerability by developing the capacity to use unilateral economic sanctions in the form of gas pricing and gas disruptions against many European North Atlantic Treaty Organization (NATO) member states. It agrees with many scholars and politicians alike who fear that Russia will leverage its monopoly of natural gas to gain political concessions. The author suggests it is only a matter of time until Russia will use natural gas as an instrument of coercion to disrupt NATO's decision-making process.

A key aim of this monograph is to explain why the rapid global transition from oil to natural gas will redefine the way policymakers and strategic security scholars look at the scarcity of natural gas in Europe. What is unique about this monograph is that it analyzes the oil and gas markets separately and illustrates, with examples, why in Europe natural gas is a more potent instrument of coercion than oil. Despite these revelations, only 1 month after the German Government announced its plans to abandon nuclear power by 2022, in July 2011 German Chancellor Angela Merkel disclosed that Germany will need to import more Russian natural gas to make up for the loss of over 10 gigawatts of generation capacity. Almost simultaneously, Germany's largest energy utilities group, RWE, and the Russian state-controlled gas giant, Gazprom, have agreed to form a strategic partnership. The author argues that situations like these create a delicate state of affairs that will ultimately undermine the de facto power of NATO in the contemporary security environment, particularly vis-à-vis Russia, unless the dependency on Russian natural gas is promptly addressed.

DOUGLAS C. LOVELACE, JR.
Director
Strategic Studies Institute

ABOUT THE AUTHOR

Alexander Ghaleb is a U.S. Army captain with several assignments to infantry, military intelligence, and special operations positions. Captain Ghaleb has written several articles dealing with issues related to national security. He has studied at top European universities in Germany, France, and Hungary. Captain Ghaleb holds a B.BA. in international business from the George Washington University, an M.A. in strategic security studies from the National Defense University, and he is an energy security Ph.D. student in the Department of Environmental Sciences and Policy at the Central European University.

SUMMARY

The nation that leads on energy will be the nation that leads the world.[1]

> David Sandalow
> The Brookings Institute

The potential for natural gas is enormous.[2]

> Barack Obama
> President of the United States

Russia enjoys vast energy and mineral resources which serve as a basis to develop its economy; as an instrument to implement domestic and foreign policy. The role of the country on international energy markets determines, in many ways, its geopolitical influence.[3]

> Vladimir Putin
> Prime Minister of the Russian
> Federation

While in the 1980s oil was considered "the only commodity whose sudden cutoff would have a drastic effect on national welfare or on economic activity,"[4] the 2030s[5] come with the image of a world in which the sudden cutoff of Russian gas to Europe will have similar disastrous effects on the economies of many European and North Atlantic Treaty Organization (NATO) member states. This monograph argues that Russian control of the natural gas supplies and of the export infrastructure systems of natural gas to Europe gives tremendous leverage to Russia in imposing its national security policy.

If in the traditional security environment the use of military force was the Union of Soviet Socialist

Republic's (USSR) preferred method of political coercion, in the contemporary security environment Russia is struggling with a weaker military that no longer represents a threat to the North Atlantic Alliance. This monograph emphasizes that Russia overcame this major vulnerability by developing the capacity to use unilateral economic sanctions in the form of gas pricing and gas disruptions against many European NATO member states. It agrees with many scholars and politicians alike who fear that Russia will leverage its monopoly of natural gas to gain political concessions;[6] and it supports the viewpoint that "Russia's energy-centered foreign policy is not limited to the states of the former Soviet Union and is clearly designed to increase its leverage in key geostrategic theaters and over United States allies."[7] While Russian officials insist that these fears are overblown, skeptics believe that "if there were a serious enough dispute, the Russians might do just that [use its energy security leverage against NATO member states]."[8]

The concerns of these skeptics cannot be dismissed without an unbiased examination of the scarcity of natural gas in the contemporary security environment, of the salience of natural gas in Russia's national security strategies, and of the natural gas pipeline politics in Eastern and Central Europe. To address these questions, the monograph has been separated into four chapters. Chapter 1 will demonstrate that like oil in the *traditional* security environment, under certain conditions, natural gas can serve as an effective unilateral instrument of state power in the *contemporary* security environment, and that its disruption by Russia will prove deadly to the economies of many NATO member states in Eastern and Central Europe (traditionally, Russia's sphere of influence). Chapter 2 will explain why Russia perceives NATO as a hostile alliance, and how Russia uses natural gas as an instrument of coercion in its sphere of influence. In Chapter 3, a look at Russia's use of natural gas as a national security instrument of coercion in negotiations with Ukraine will help energy security analysts determine the conditions under which Russia will leverage its energy superpower position in its relations with European Union (EU) and/or NATO member states. Additionally, a look at Russia's failures in the use of such coercion in Ukraine will assist NATO member states in Eastern and Central Europe to identify ways to reduce the threat of disruption of Russian gas supplies. Finally, Chapter 4 will expose the processes Russia uses in the context of natural gas negotiations to bribe Western European nations—such as Germany, France, and Italy—to divide the NATO Alliance, and to rule over its traditional sphere of influence in Eastern and Central Europe.

To avoid digressing into general theory, this monograph also makes one significant assumption: that unless new alternative energy sources emerge, natural gas will surpass oil by year 2050[9] and will grow to become the fuel of the future. While there is enough body of evidence to illustrate this, some of which is discussed in Chapter 1, it is not my purpose to enter into ideological arguments on the future global production and demand for natural gas. I will, instead, focus on the energy security implications of the current "global shift to gas,"[10] and on how this move will change the way we look at Russia in the contemporary security environment.

Finally, given time and space constraints, this monograph will not be able to proffer solutions to Russia's fast ascent to great-power status. However, the conclusion will address several recommendations and implications requiring further research as a starting point for policymakers and national defense officials in their search for comprehensive answers to Europe and NATO's growing dependency on Russian natural gas.

ENDNOTES - SUMMARY

1. David Sandalow, "Keynote Speech to Battery Technology for Transportation: From Scientific Discovery to Marketplace Event," Washington, DC: The Brookings Institution, February 8, 2011.

2. Bryan Walsh, "The Gas Dilemma," (Cover Story), *Time*, Vol. 177, No. 14, April 11, 2011, p. 42.

3. Roman Kupchinsky, "LNG--Russia's New Energy Blackmail Tool," *Eurasia Daily Monitor*, Vol. 6, No. 77, April 22, 2009.

4. Richard H. Ullman, "Redefining Security," The MIT Press, *International Security*, Vol. 8, No. 1, Summer, 1983, p. 144.

5. *Flexibility in Natural Gas Supply and Demand*, Paris, France: Organization for Economic Cooperation and Development (OECD)/International Energy Agency (IEA), 2002; Joe Barnes *et al.*, "Introduction to the Study," David G. Victor, Amy M. Jaffe, and Mark H. Hayes, eds., *Natural Gas and Geopolitics from 1970 to 2040*, New York: Cambridge University Press, 2006, p. 3.

6. Jeffrey Mankoff, *Eurasian Energy Security*, Washington, DC: Council on Foreign Relations, 2009; Roman Kupchinsky, "LNG - Russia's New Energy Blackmail Tool," *Eurasia Daily Monitor*, Vol. 6, No. 77, April 22, 2009.

7. Anita Orbán, *Power, Energy, and the New Russian Imperialism*, Westport, CT: Praeger Security International, 2008, p. 177.

8. Marshall Goldman, *Petrostate: Putin, Power, and the New Russia*, New York: Oxford University Press, 2008, p. 158.

9. Barnes *et al.*, p. 3.

10. *Ibid.*, p. 4.

CHAPTER 1

REDEFINING THE SCARCITY OF NATURAL GAS IN THE CONTEMPORARY SECURITY ENVIRONMENT

Natural gas will be the currency through which energy-rich countries leverage their interests against import dependent nations. The use of energy as an overt weapon is not a theoretical threat of the future; it is happening now.[1]

Senator Richard "Dick" Lugar

The purpose of this chapter is to show why natural gas can be used as an effective instrument of unilateral sanctions in the contemporary security environment.[2] This issue is important not only because energy security[3] is an integral part of any state's national security, but also because the scarcity of natural resources has been proven to create dependencies that could cripple a nation's economic development. Of course, a strong economy depends not only on natural resources; but it is an indisputable fact that without access to natural resources, national industries and economies cannot grow. Under the right conditions, severing access to vital natural resources, such as oil, can also lead to imminent economic decline. This has already been demonstrated by the oil crises of the traditional security environment,[4] which had devastating effects on the economies of both developing and developed nations. A clear example is the 1973 Arab Oil Embargo, when a mere 7-percent cut in oil supply had a profound impact on both economies and consumers.[5] The purpose of this chapter is to show how the two conditions—political and economic—that arise from the nature of the natural gas global market and players make natural gas a potent tool of coercion for energy superstates, such as Russia. Furthermore, while the tendency of many scholars in the energy security field has been to analyze a nation's dependency on oil and gas together, this chapter will analyze the two energy markets separately. This is an attempt to determine if natural gas is a more potent instrument of coercion in the contemporary security environment than oil was in the traditional security environment.

Until recently, never in history have unilateral sanctions of gas disruptions been successfully employed. The notion that nation states, if given the opportunity, will resort to using economic statecraft to address foreign policy disputes is not new; it can be traced back in history all the way to 432 BC and the Megarian decree.[6] However, the notion that energy superstates, such as Russia, will leverage their neighbors' scarcity of natural gas and attempt to use unilateral economic sanctions for political ends is a new concept, and one that does not have the full support of academia.[7] While some scholars recognize that unilateral sanctions can be successful when high dependency and lack of expedient alternatives to replace this dependency exist,[8] there are almost no examples presented in more recent academic literature to support the supposition that gas disruptions acted as the main instruments of coercion.

ON DISAGREEMENTS INVOLVING THE THEORY OF UNILATERAL ECONOMIC SANCTIONS

Many of the disagreements between political scholars emerge from the use of definitions. Vague uses of terminology and ambiguous definitions almost always produce disputable conclusions. This treatise will adopt Steve Chan's definition of sanctions as "the actual or threatened withdrawal of economic resources to affect a policy change by the target,"[9] and will complement that definition with that of Ivan Eland, who sees the purpose of sanctions "to have the maximum political effect through introducing psychological pressure against its political leaders and populace."[10]

Despite the arguments of political science scholars like Edward Mansfield,[11] Johan Galtung,[12] and George T. Doran,[13] who argue against the use of sanctions as tools of foreign policy, this treatise belongs to the "unilateral sanctions can work" school of thought. This treatise also argues that under certain political and economic conditions, unilateral sanctions "can indeed work in terms of influencing the policies of the actor against which they are ostensibly targeted."[14] While the utility of sanctions was favored by many political scientists—most notably David Mitrany[15] and Albert Hirschman;[16] and more recently by Gary Hufbauer, Jeffrey Schott, and Kimberly Elliott (HSE)[17]—my argument is that under certain conditions unilateral sanctions can represent even better instruments of coercion than multilateral sanctions. Thus, I disagree with scholars like Barfield and Groombridge,[18] who assert that only multilateral sanctions ought to be considered by policymakers. In fact, recent research shows that the success rate of economic sanctions decreases when sanctions are multilateral, multi-issue, and when no international institution is present.[19]

This monograph will not attempt to challenge the belief that multilateral sanctions "almost never work."[20] Instead, it agrees with the estimate of Hossein Askari, who writes that "the idea that economic sanctions can address foreign policy issues without military action requires a host of requisite economic and political conditions that are rarely found in the world in the right combination and at the right time."[21] More specifically, multilateral sanctions require a coalition with the political will and the economic power to impose the sanctions. Because this is the case, there are two main reasons depicted in academic literature to explain why multilateral sanctions more often than not fail: failure to agree on the strategic purpose of imposed sanctions (thus, a political consideration); and the differential cost of sanctions among the senders (largely an economic factor).

First, allies hardly ever agree on the objective of imposed sanctions. David Baldwin writes that "neither war nor economics can be divorced from politics; each must be judged as an instrument serving the higher goals of the polity";[22] economic sanctions are no exception to this rule. If the purpose of sanctions is "to affect a policy change by the target,"[23] then senders (the countries imposing the sanctions)[24] must determine which policy the target (the immediate object of the sanctions episode)[25] is expected to change. Since each sender has different reasons to impose sanctions on the target (causing a conflict of the ends), and since only rarely do these motives coincide with those of the other senders,[26] reaching an agreement on imposing multilateral sanctions is extremely hard to realize.

Second, the cost of imposing sanctions is simply greater for some sender states than the potential benefits brought upon by the sanctions.[27] Winston Churchill once said that "the inherent vice of capitalism is the unequal sharing of blessings"[28]; and this is also the case with the benefits of imposing economic sanctions. There are times when the costs of imposing sanctions are just too high to bear by the sender. HSE determined that the relative cost to the sender can be classified in one of four categories: "net gain to the sender" (usually the case when only aid is withheld); "little effect on sender" (when insignificant trade disruptions occur); "modest loss to sender" (when trade is lost, but the loss is not substantial); and "major loss to sender" (when loss of trade adversely affects the sender's economy).[29] Each sender fits into one of the categories listed above, and in the case of multilateral sanctions, almost never do they fit in the same category. Because this is the case, senders that incur a major loss as a result of the sanctions are more likely to stop supporting the sanctions — causing their implementation to fail.

As seen above, and almost every time, the failure of multilateral sanctions lies with the sender states, and not with the instruments of coercion (the means). This is not the case with unilateral sanctions. Some scholars wrongly assume that if an agreement cannot be reached on multilateral sanctions, then, logically, unilateral sanctions will also fail, because if unilateral sanctions are imposed, there is no guarantee that the target will not simply circumvent the sender by trading with other states.[30] The problem with this argument is that it does not apply to situations in which the sender has a monopoly on the instruments of coercion. As we will see later in this monograph, Russia's monopoly of the gas supply to Eastern Europe allows it to impose unilateral sanctions at will, without the fear that the target will attempt to get gas from other European states (simply because the other European states also get much of their gas from Russia). In fact, empirical evidence[31] derived from the HSE data set (a total of 115 cases between 1970 and 1990),[32] as well as from the Threat and Imposition of Sanctions (TIES) data set developed by T. Clifton Morgan (a total of 888 cases from 1971-2000)[33] "demonstrate convincingly and consistently that multilateral sanctions were less effective than unilateral sanctions,"[34] and that under certain conditions, unilateral economic sanctions can act as successful tools of state power. This fact also explains why oil consistently failed to be used as an instrument of coercion against Western Europe in the past, because no one state holds the monopoly of supply and transportation of oil to Europe.[35]

The monopoly or near-monopoly of the sources of a critical energy supply not only satisfies the main economic condition for imposing unilateral sanctions, but also creates an environment in which the sender state can afford to impose economic sanctions without having to rely on a coalition of senders with conflicting political objectives—resolving the main political condition that is not satisfied by multilateral sanctions. As we will see in later chapters, Russia's monopoly of the sources of natural gas to most of Eastern and Central Europe allows Russia to impose sanctions as a single state, because it does not have the same coordination and differential cost problems of a multilateral coalition of senders.

Compared to natural gas, the economic and political conditions to impose unilateral sanctions were, however, rarely present for oil. While crude oil markets have had disruptions in the past, almost none of them have been politically motivated,[36] and when they were, they only served to disprove the coercive potential of oil.[37] In fact, Harvard University's Rosemary Kelanic[38] insisted that there are no examples in history in which oil was successfully used as an instrument of coercion,[39] arguing that the global market for oil is structured to exacerbate the difficulties of imposing economic sanctions.[40]

OIL AS THE DOMINANT STRATEGIC RESOURCE OF THE TRADITIONAL SECURITY ENVIRONMENT

We know today that coal fueled the Industrial Revolution during most of the 19th century, resulting in unprecedented economic growth for both the European and the North American continents. The shift to oil started on the brink of the 20th century, when Lord Bearsted — the head of Shell Transport and Trading Company — succeeded in convincing Winston Churchill that switching from coal to oil would strengthen the British Navy. Indeed, the shift to oil proved to be most advantageous for Britain during World War I, when the Royal Navy managed to outmaneuver the German High Seas Fleet, because it was using oil as opposed to coal.[41] The United States followed suit in recognizing the potential of oil; not only for military purposes, but for economic purposes as well. It could be argued today that without the oil supply glut of the early-20th century, the Ford Model T would never have become an affordable option for America's middle class.

The glut ended, however, with the start of World War I, when the attention of policymakers shifted to the scarcity of oil; to the possibility that national oil reserves might actually run out at one point in the future. Despite these concerns, oil replaced coal as the energy of choice in both Europe and North America by the mid-20th century. Dependency of the industrialized world on oil increased to such an extent, that by 1967 disruption of oil supplies from Saudi Arabia, Iraq, Kuwait, and Libya[42] for 3 months would have cost the United Kingdom £1.2 billion, almost crippling its economy.[43]

The "oil weapon" concept appeared for the first time in 1935, when the League of Nations unsuccessfully considered multilateral economic sanctions against Italy.[44] Only a few years later, in 1941, the United States (which was holding a near-monopoly on the supply of oil to Japan) successfully imposed an oil embargo on Japan for its incursion into China (the first recorded time that oil was used as an instrument of coercion). This gave Japan only 18 months to defeat the United States before the exhaustion of its domestic reserves, which would have led to a complete economic collapse. The Japan episode proved that oil can be used as an instrument of coercion when the sender can restrict access to most of the oil supply to the target (the United States successfully restricted 80 percent of Japan's oil supply).[45] The U.S. capacity to restrict Japan's military plans by imposing this new type of unilateral sanction influenced Adolf Hitler to state (in Finland, June 1942) that he could not have attacked Russia without access to the Romanian oil supplies.[46]

An attempt to use oil as an instrument of coercion against Western Europe and the United States was demonstrated during the 1973 Arab Oil Embargo, when Saudi Arabia, Egypt, Syria, and the Persian Gulf sheikhdoms attempted to lessen the American support for Israel by imposing an oil embargo.[47] But the use of multilateral sanctions failed in 1973. On March 17, 1974, less than 6 months after it was imposed, the embargo was lifted because of multiple disagreements between sender states;[48] indicating how hard it is to use oil as an instrument of coercion. This is particularly true if we consider the "strategic deficits of prospective weapon users"[49] (the lack of agreement between oil-producing countries), and the ease in circumventing the sanctions if they are unilaterally imposed.[50]

Given the lessons learned from oil in the traditional security environment, it may surprise many to discover that in the contemporary security environment, the problems with using oil as a sanction are not as acute with natural gas. If the global market for oil is structured to exacerbate the problems with using oil as sanction (largely because the oil market is a demand issue more than it is a supply issue),[51] the global market for natural gas is structured to alleviate these problems, because the flexibility in the transportation of natural gas differs significantly from the flexibility in the transportation of oil.

GAS IS BECOMING THE DOMINANT STRATEGIC RESOURCE FOR THE CONTEMPORARY SECURITY ENVIRONMENT

If the developed economies in the 19th century were fueled by coal, and in the 20th century by oil, the 21st century comes with great promise for natural gas.[52] The world's energy markets are experiencing a rapid transition to gas[53] that will incontrovertibly redefine the way we look at the scarcity of natural gas in the contemporary security environment. Recent discoveries of natural gas fields and developments in exploitation capabilities already make natural gas the most readily available fossil fuel on the planet.[54] According to the chief executive officer of Royal Dutch Shell, Peter Voser, "there's now enough technically recoverable gas in the ground [worldwide] for 250 years at current production rates."[55] This abundance[56] of supply means that availability and/or scarcity of natural gas worldwide are no longer determinants of energy insecurity. Instead, in recent years, fears of imminent shortages have been replaced by fears of dependencies on foreign gas suppliers,[57] and by regional concerns about the lack of natural gas infrastructure.[58]

These concerns will continue to grow as dependence on natural gas deepens. Natural gas is currently the world's third leading energy source in terms of consumption and production, and is expected to replace coal as the number one fuel for generating electric power in the next several years.[59] Global consumption is rising faster than any other primary energy source, and projections show that consumption will double in the next 2 decades.[60] If this rate of growth remains constant, natural gas will become the world's most important primary energy source by year 2050, surpassing both coal and oil.[61]

Environmental,[62] economic,[63] technological,[64] and even geostrategic[65] considerations indicate that this increase in both consumption and production of natural gas will not be inhibited in the coming years. First, from an environmental perspective, worldwide efforts to limit emissions of carbon dioxide[66] and greenhouse gas[67] mean the importance of natural gas will continue to grow.[68] Natural gas is the cleanest-burning fossil fuel per unit of energy;[69] its efficient combustion translates into a considerable drop in carbon emissions.[70]

Second, from an economic perspective, cheaper natural gas (relative to the cost of oil) translates into cheaper electricity.[71] Academic research shows that cheaper gas results in a positive correlation between natural gas consumption and economic growth.[72] As top economists from the International Energy Agency (IEA) are predicting a supply glut in the coming years,[73] the price of gas will continue to go down until an economic equilibrium is reached.[74] This trend also led to the emergence of the natural gas vehicles (NGVs). Acknowledging the coming shift to gas, some automobile makers have now started to develop natural gas powered cars. The 2011 Honda Civic GX is only the first to be sold by a major automaker. Before the Civic GX hit the market, however, there were already 10 million natural gas vehicles worldwide.[75] With 70 percent of U.S. demand for oil resulting from the transportation sector,[76] the emergence of the NGVs will also result in a decreased demand for oil and an increased demand for natural gas. Reports say an NGV translates into lower fuel costs, and there is almost no difference in performance, when compared with the gasoline-powered model:[77]

> For drivers, natural-gas refueling costs are about one-third less than that for gasoline. Equally important, there is reportedly little difference in acceleration, mileage, and performance between natural gas and similar gasoline-powered vehicles.[78]

Third, technological advances[79] in the extraction methodologies and the emergence of unconventional gas reserves (i.e., the "Shale Gas Revolution")[80] are also expected to play a major role in the increase of production. Daniel Yergin,[81] co-founder and chairman of Cambridge Energy Research Associates, calls

11

the extraction capabilities of natural gas from shale (a technique known as "fracking")[82] "the biggest innovation in fossil fuel resource development since the start of the 21st century,"[83] and suggests that current projections[84] of unconventional gas production are conservative at best.

Finally, as the emergence of a society dependent on natural gas becomes more apparent, it has been wrongly assumed that because the "locations of gas reserves are more diversified regionally than oil,"[85] gas supplies are also more reliable than oil. This argument ignores, however, the lack of flexibility in the transportation of natural gas and the over-reliance of most developing countries on natural gas supplies by pipeline. Because of this, unilateral sanctions using natural gas cannot be avoided if the sender has a monopoly on the supply by pipeline, and if the target does not have access to a constant supply of liquefied natural gas (LNG) as an alternative.[86] If unilateral sanctions using oil are doomed to fail — as discussed previously, because of the ease in circumventing the sender of such sanctions — the corollary is that unilateral sanctions using natural gas will succeed if the target has no way of circumventing these sanctions.

WHY NATURAL GAS CAN SERVE AS AN EFFECTIVE, UNILATERAL INSTRUMENT OF STATE POWER

In June of 2003, Alan Greenspan — who served as Chairman of the Federal Reserve of the United States from 1987 to 2006 — testified before the U.S. House of Representatives' Committee on Energy and Commerce that while natural gas reserves are more diversified globally than oil,[87] limited capacity for LNG imports can effectively inhibit a state's access to the world's abundant reserves of natural gas.[88] According to Greenspan, because the natural gas market depends highly on the use of pipelines, the "inability to increase imports to close a modest gap between North American demand and production (a gap we can almost always close in oil)"[89] was, in fact, the reason the U.S. price of gas for delivery in July 2003[90] was almost double the price for delivery in July of the previous year.[91] This inflexibility of the natural gas transportation system, said Greenspan, is not present in the transportation of oil:[92]

> Such pressures do not arise in the U.S. market for crude oil. American refiners have unlimited access to world supplies, as was demonstrated most recently when Venezuelan oil production shut down. Refiners were able to replace lost oil with supplies from Europe, Asia, and the Middle East. If North American natural gas markets are to function with the flexibility exhibited by oil, unlimited access to the vast world reserves of gas is required. Markets need to be able to effectively adjust to unexpected shortfalls in domestic supply. Access to world natural gas supplies will require a major expansion of LNG terminal import capacity. Without the flexibility such facilities will impart, imbalances in supply and demand must inevitably engender price volatility.[93]

Not surprisingly, since Greenspan's testimony, the United States has been trying to balance its supply and demand of natural gas by decreasing its dependence on natural gas imports by pipeline. To this effect, shale gas production increased 14-fold over the last decade,[94] while LNG imports have continued to grow (though at a much slower pace). Furthermore, the U.S. Energy Information Administration is projecting that imports of LNG will steadily increase "from current levels of around 2.5% of total natural gas consumption to 12.4% by 2030,"[95] further underlining the significance of LNG in increasing the flexibility of the natural gas transportation system. Ultimately, the current inflexibility highlights the negative effects that the dependency on natural gas pipelines can have on the well-being of states, and the latter's inability to circumvent this instrument of coercion if the sender holds a monopoly on the supply of natural gas by pipeline, and no access to LNG is available to the target.

The problem with LNG, however, is that it "requires a complex and extremely expensive infrastructure to link the source to final consumption."[96] The IEA, estimated that the United States alone had to invest half-a-trillion dollars in LNG infrastructure to fill the gap between current demand and supply,[97] which was hard to come by, illustrating the fact that "regasification capacity is no longer and perhaps never was the constraining factor for U.S. LNG imports. The constraint now is willingness to pay."[98] Clearly, most developing countries around the world cannot afford to make this kind of investment in order to respond to unexpected natural gas disruptions.[99] This effectively making certain states — particularly in Eastern and Central Europe — potential targets of coercion, especially if they have no access to LNG, and if the sender is the sole supplier of natural gas by pipeline to the target.[100]

REDEFINING NATURAL GAS AS AN EFFECTIVE TOOL OF UNILATERAL SANCTIONS IN EASTERN AND CENTRAL EUROPE

As with oil, Europe has access to very limited domestic reserves of natural gas. In fact, the consumption of natural gas in most European countries depends entirely on natural gas imports (see Figure 1-1). Furthermore, nine European countries (Finland, Lithuania, Latvia, Estonia, Slovakia, Bulgaria, the Czech Republic, Hungary, and Greece) rely almost entirely on Russian gas. On average, at least 85 percent of their domestic natural gas consumption is supplied by Russia.[101] The inflexibility in the transportation of natural gas to Eastern and Central Europe satisfies both the necessary and sufficient economic and political conditions for Russia to successfully employ natural gas as a unilateral instrument of coercion in this region (whereas this was not the case with oil). The corollary, as we will see later in this monograph, is that "Russia has already revealed its willingness to withhold natural gas supply based on political disagreements."[102] Thus, the concern in Europe—and rightfully so—has been that Russia's monopoly of natural gas from the Caucasus will impact Europe's energy security.

In Western Europe, there are currently 15 operational LNG terminals located across eight countries,[103] and no one country holds a monopoly of natural gas by pipeline. Despite this, Western European nations are planning on adding 65 billion cubic meters (bcm) to the current 68 bcm in LNG import capacity over the next decade (representing 19.6 percent of the over 676 bcm of natural gas per year that will be imported to Continental Europe by 2020).[104] This increase in LNG imports is due mainly to concerns about Europe's increasing dependence on gas by pipeline, which remains evident in current statistics, showing that by 2030, the European Union (EU) will import over 60 percent of its natural gas by pipeline from Russia alone.[105] Dependency on Russian gas by pipeline is expected to rise because of a forecasted decrease in domestic gas production, and an estimated increase

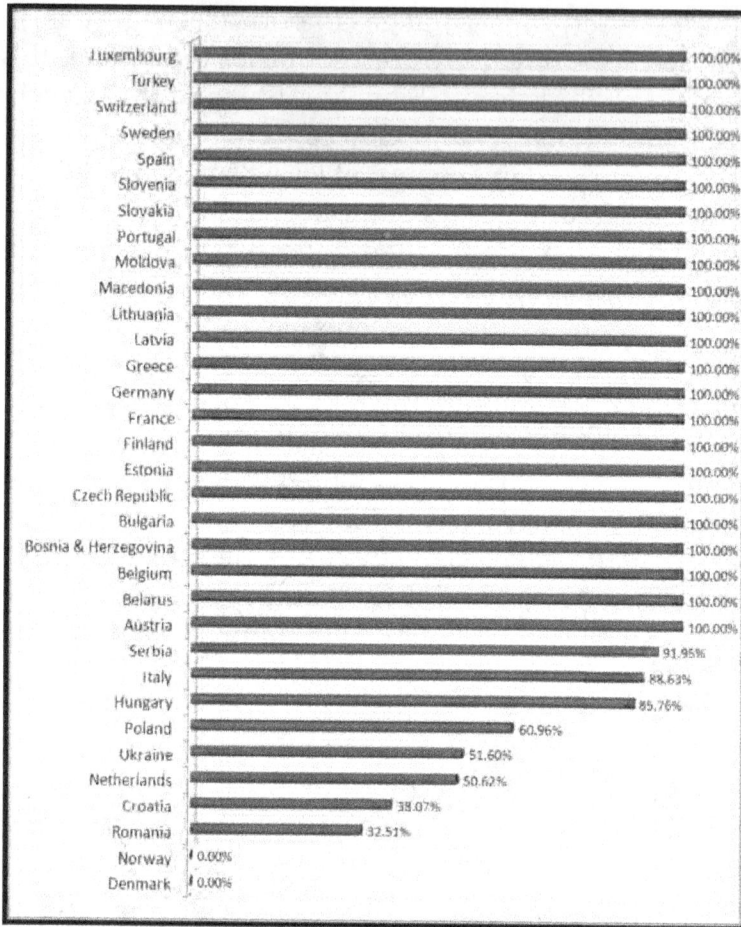

Country	Percentage
Luxembourg	100.00%
Turkey	100.00%
Switzerland	100.00%
Sweden	100.00%
Spain	100.00%
Slovenia	100.00%
Slovakia	100.00%
Portugal	100.00%
Moldova	100.00%
Macedonia	100.00%
Lithuania	100.00%
Latvia	100.00%
Greece	100.00%
Germany	100.00%
France	100.00%
Finland	100.00%
Estonia	100.00%
Czech Republic	100.00%
Bulgaria	100.00%
Bosnia & Herzegovina	100.00%
Belgium	100.00%
Belarus	100.00%
Austria	100.00%
Serbia	91.95%
Italy	88.63%
Hungary	85.76%
Poland	60.96%
Ukraine	51.60%
Netherlands	50.62%
Croatia	38.07%
Romania	32.51%
Norway	0.00%
Denmark	0.00%

Source: Eurostat energy statistics; author's calculations.

Figure 1-1. Europe's Dependency on Natural Gas Imports By Country (2009 Estimate).

in consumption of gas in Organization for Economic Cooperation and Development (OECD) Europe by 87 percent by 2030.[106] This places natural gas right behind oil as Europe's total primary energy supply (TPES).[107]

The dependency of Eastern and Central Europe (ECE) on natural gas imports is, however, of even greater concern. Often viewed as the periphery of the EU, but also as an important transit corridor for gas to many North Atlantic Treaty Organization (NATO) members, ECE is today the most important "battle space" of the "energy war."[108] Centrally positioned between the Moscow-Berlin-Rome-Paris Energy Axis in Europe[109] and the growing Russia-China-Iran Energy Nexus in Asia,[110] ECE arguably holds the power to consolidate Russia's monopoly on energy supplies to Europe. As noted in the previous section, for most countries in ECE, almost all imports of natural gas are supplied by Russia. Without the Nabucco pipeline,[111] the Russian control of gas supplies to ECE will exceed 91 percent by 2020 (see Figure 1-2);[112] Romania and Poland are the only ECE countries that will have access to domestic production and LNG supplies.

Source: The values for the chart above originate from Lajtai's report to the 24th World Gas Conference. Buenos Aires, Argentina, October 6-9, 2009; author's representation.

Figure 1-2. Projected Russian Control of Natural Gas Supplies in Eastern and Central Europe.

Despite these serious trends, and contrary to data that show that Europe will "become hostage to yet another vital energy source,"[113] Russian-American economist and Harvard University Professor Andrei Shleifer[114] and UCLA Professor of Political Science Daniel Treisman[115] disagree with these concerns: "Has the dependence on Russian gas given Moscow political leverage over countries to the west? There is little sign of this."[116] The two scholars argue that there is little evidence to suggest "a more sinister design in the Kremlin's foreign policy: to reimpose Russian hegemony over the former Soviet states, and perhaps an even greater portion of Eastern Europe, by means of economic and military pressure."[117] Their main argument is an economic one; that Russia needs to sell its gas to Europe more than Europe needs to buy it:

> It is Russia's dependence on the European market — and not the other way around — that is most striking. Europe, including the Baltic states, is the destination for about 67 percent of Russia's gas exports (other former Soviet countries buy the other 33 percent). . . . Given the extent to which Russia's income and budget depend on this trade, losing its European clients would be a calamity.[118]

Shleifer and Treisman argued that in fact "Russia has been in geopolitical retreat over the last 20 years,"[119] and that the LNG market and the shale gas revolution knocked Russia's gas industry "off balance."[120] This has also been the view of various Capitol Hill officials — who have been interviewed in Washington, DC, by the author of this monograph — and that of former U.S. Undersecretary of Energy John Deutch, who wrote that the results of the current natural gas revolution will be that "countries that export large amounts of natural gas will suffer from lower than expected revenues and a reduced ability to use energy as a tool of foreign policy."[121] Furthermore, scholarly papers and scientific reports (like a 2010 report by IHS Cambridge Energy Research Associates)[122] suggest that decreased reliance on Middle Eastern resources could in fact enhance each region's energy security;[123] and that "natural gas is not being affected by the global-geopolitical winds."[124] In Europe, however, their conclusions could not be further from the truth.

First, Shleifer and Treisman are fundamentally wrong in their assessment that Russia needs to sell its gas to Europe more than Europe needs to buy it, because currently Europe does not have a united energy front nor an integrated energy market and infrastructure.[125] Because of this, each European country must be looked at independently in its energy trade relations with Russia. If this is the case, clearly, many ECE countries need to import the Russian natural gas more than Russia needs to sell it to them (see Figure 1-3).[126] For example, 100 percent of Lithuania's natural gas imports come from Russia, but that amounts to only 1.97 percent of total Russian natural gas exports. That means that if Russia decides to cut the supply of natural gas to Lithuania, the Lithuanian people may end up having a very cold winter, while Russia will simply recuperate its losses by slightly increasing its natural gas exports to other European nations.

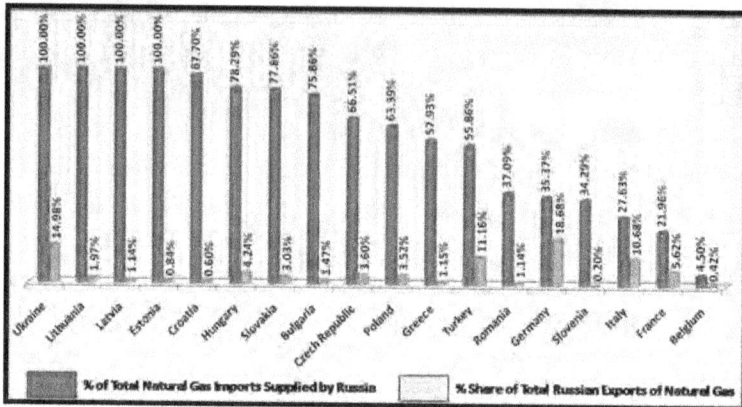

% of Total Natural Gas Imports Supplied by Russia   % Share of Total Russian Exports of Natural Gas

Source: Eurostat energy statistics; author's calculations.

Figure 1-3. Tearing Down the Myth of "Interdependency" between European NATO Member States (Plus Ukraine) and Russia (2009 Estimate).

Second, the LNG market did nothing to knock Russia's gas industry "off balance," as Shleifer and Treisman argue. While LNG represents only 20 percent of the European natural gas market,[127] it is currently available only to Western Europe.[128] Furthermore, the only LNG projects in ECE that are currently being considered have been initiated by the two ECE countries that depend the least on natural gas imports: Romania and Poland; these projects represent only 2.3 percent of the natural gas that will be imported to Continental Europe by 2020. The Swinoujscie LNG terminal will supply Poland with 7.5 bcm per year by 2018;[129] while the AGRI—Azerbaijan-Georgia-Romania Interconnector—will supply Romania with 8 bcm per year.[130] The rest of the Eastern and Central European nations will remain almost entirely dependent on Russian gas and, as shown in this chapter, will remain potential targets of unilateral sanctions.

Finally, shale gas will not reduce Russia's ability to use natural gas as a tool of foreign policy in Europe, as John Deutch proposes. While shale deposits[131] are available all over the globe, "there are no reliable estimates about the size of the economically recoverable shale resource base worldwide."[132] For example, in Europe, companies are currently developing shale gas operations only in Germany, Poland, and Romania,[133] and there is no indication that similar operations will begin in other ECE countries. Furthermore, recovery of unconventional gas reserves like shale gas is expected to be very limited in Europe due to environmental challenges:

> Communities are especially concerned about the fracking fluid — that it uses too much water (a typical well may require 3-4 million gallons), that it will not be cleaned up, that it contaminates drinking water, and that the chemicals used in it have not been publicly disclosed."[134]

For the sake of argument, it could also be easily assumed that since Russia did not use oil as an instrument of unilateral sanctions in the traditional security environment, similarly, it will not use natural gas as an instrument of unilateral sanctions in the traditional security environment either. However, while oil and gas seem to be impacting Europe's energy security equally, this chapter has shown that the inflexibility in the transportation of natural gas to ECE satisfies both the necessary and sufficient economic and political conditions for Russia to employ natural gas successfully as an unilateral instrument of coercion in this region (whereas this was not the case with oil).[135] Indeed, over the past decade and in the absence of LNG supplies, the fear has been that the country that controls the supply of natural gas by pipeline from the Caucasus (Russia) will be in position of imposing unilateral sanctions if and when it so desires. Because of these concerns, EU Energy Commissioner Günther Oettinger admitted in 2011 that "the energy challenge is one of the greatest tests"[136] for Europe.

To illustrate these concerns further, I have developed a metric for susceptibility to Russian coercion (see Figure 1-4) that takes into consideration the share of TPES representing Russian natural gas (from Figure 1-5),[137] the asymmetry in diversification of natural gas trade partners (from Figure 1-3), the share of trade deficit as a percentage of total trade with Russia (from Figure 1-6),[138] minus the share of Russia's world trade occupied by each country inserted into the metric (see Table 1-1). The metric developed ranks Lithuania as the country most susceptible to Russian coercion; Germany ranks as the least susceptible. Not surprisingly, in March 2011, Lithuanian Energy Minister Arvydas Sekmokas accused Russia of putting "political and economic pressure" on the Lithuanian government.[139] Russia stands accused of charging Lithuania higher rates than any other EU country as a "punishment" for taking steps to break away from Russia's natural gas monopoly.[140] Unfortunately, it may take Lithuania and other ECE countries years, if not decades, to break free from their dependency on Russian natural gas. Because of this, a current report published by the Council on Foreign Relations goes as far as to conclude that "no magic bullet will rescue Europe from its dependence on Russia for the foreseeable future."[141]

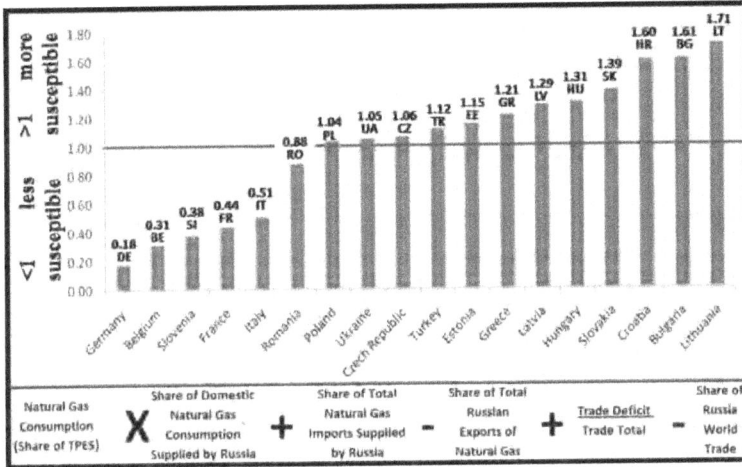

Sources: Enerdata, CIA Factbook, Gazprom Export LLC, DG Trade, and Eurostat energy statistics; author's calculations.

Figure 1-4. Levels of Susceptibility to Russian Coercion among European NATO Member States and Ukraine (2009 Estimate).[142]

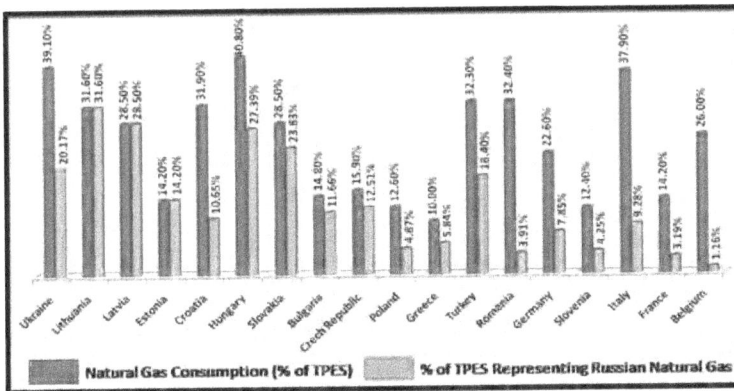

Figure 1-5. Share of TPES Russian Natural Gas Holds in European NATO Member States and Ukraine (2009 Estimate).

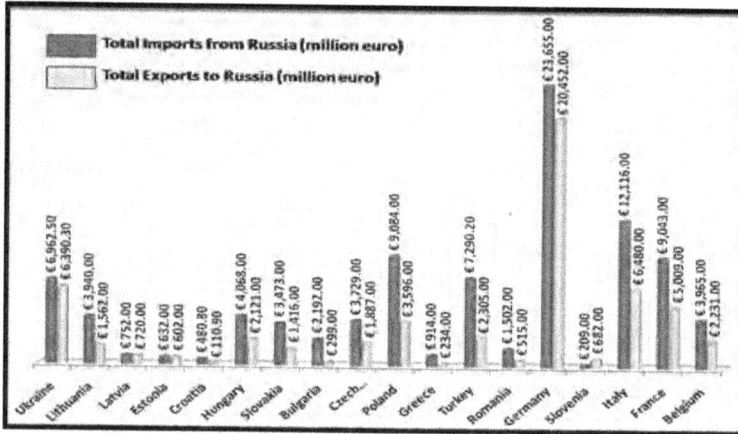

Source: Eurostat energy statistics; author's calculations.

Figure 1-6. Balance of Trade with Russia (2009 Estimate).

Country	Natural Gas Consumption (% of TPES)	Proven Natural Gas Reserves (BCM)	Domestic Production of Natural Gas (BCM)	Domestic Consumption of Natural Gas (BCM)	Export of Natural Gas (BCM)	Import of Natural Gas (BCM)	% Dependency on Natural Gas Imports	Imports of Natural Gas Supplied by Russia (BCM)	% of Total Natural Gas Imports Supplied by Russia	% of Domestic Natural Gas Consumption Supplied by Russia	% Share of Total Russian Exports of Natural Gas
Ukraine	39.10%	1104	21.2	52	5	26.83	51.60%	26.83	100.00%	51.60%	14.98%
Lithuania	31.60%	0	0	3.53	0	3.53	100.00%	3.53	100.00%	100.00%	1.97%
Latvia	28.50%	0	0	2.05	0	2.05	100.00%	2.05	100.00%	100.00%	1.14%
Estonia	14.20%	0	0	1.51	0	1.51	100.00%	1.51	100.00%	100.00%	0.84%
Croatia	31.90%	30.58	2.847	3.205	0.695	1.22	38.07%	1.07	87.70%	33.39%	0.60%
Hungary	40.80%	8.098	2.603	11.32	0.085	9.708	85.76%	7.6	78.29%	67.14%	4.24%
Slovakia	28.50%	14.16	0.103	6.493	0.015	6.974	107.41%	5.43	77.86%	83.63%	3.03%
Bulgaria	14.80%	5.663	0.218	3.35	0	3.48	103.88%	2.64	75.86%	78.81%	1.47%
Czech Republic	15.90%	3.964	0.176	8.182	1.111	9.683	118.35%	6.44	66.51%	78.71%	3.60%
Poland	12.60%	164.8	5.842	16.33	0.04	9.954	60.96%	6.31	63.39%	38.64%	3.52%
Greece	10.00%	0.991	0.009	3.528	0	3.556	100.79%	2.06	57.93%	58.39%	1.15%
Turkey	32.30%	6.088	1.014	35.07	0.708	35.77	102.00%	19.98	55.86%	56.97%	11.16%
Romania	32.40%	63	11.42	16.92	0	5.5	32.51%	2.04	37.09%	12.06%	1.14%
Germany	22.60%	175.6	15.29	96.26	12.64	94.57	98.24%	33.45	35.37%	34.75%	18.68%
Slovenia	12.40%	0	0	1.05	0	1.05	100.00%	0.36	34.29%	34.29%	0.20%
Italy	37.90%	69.83	8.12	78.12	0.124	69.24	88.63%	19.13	27.63%	24.49%	10.68%
France	14.20%	7.079	0.877	44.84	1.931	45.85	102.25%	10.07	21.96%	22.46%	5.62%
Belgium	26.00%	0	0	16.87	0	16.78	99.47%	0.7551	4.50%	4.48%	0.42%
SOURCE:	ENERDATA/ EUROSTAT			CIA FACTBOOK					Gazprom Export LLC & CIA Factbook		

			% EU27/World
Russian Total Natural Gas Exports (BCM)	179.1		
Russian Total Exports (million euro)	€ 202,240.80	Russian Exports to EU 27 (million euro)	€ 115,408.00	57.06%
Russian Total Imports (million euro)	€ 113,817.91	Russian Imports from EU 27 (million euro)	€ 65,660.00	57.69%
Russia World Trade (million euro)	€ 316,058.71	Russia - EU27 Total Trade (million euro)	€ 181,068.00	57.29%
Trade Balance in Favor of Russia (million euro)	€ 88,422.89	Trade Balance in Favor of Russia (million euro)	€ 49,748.00	56.26%

Source: Enerdata, CIA *Factbook*, Gazprom Export LLC, DG Trade; and Eurostat energy statistics; author's calculations.

Table 1-1. NATO Member States in Continental Europe Plus Ukraine: Trade with Russia Statistics (2009 Estimate).

Country	Total Imports from Russia (million euro)	% Share of Total Russian Exports (million euro)	Total Exports to Russia (million euro)	Trade Total (million euro)	% of Russia World Trade	Trade Deficit (million euro)	Level of Susceptibility
Ukraine	6,962.50 €	3.44%	6,390.30 €	13,352.80 €	4.22%	572.20 €	1.05
Lithuania	3,940.00 €	1.95%	1,562.00 €	5,502.00 €	1.74%	2,378.00 €	1.71
Latvia	752.00 €	0.37%	720.00 €	1,472.00 €	0.47%	32.00 €	1.29
Estonia	632.00 €	0.31%	602.00 €	1,234.00 €	0.39%	30.00 €	1.15
Croatia	480.80 €	0.24%	110.90 €	591.70 €	0.19%	369.90 €	1.60
Hungary	4,068.00 €	2.01%	2,121.00 €	6,189.00 €	1.96%	1,947.00 €	1.31
Slovakia	3,473.00 €	1.72%	1,416.00 €	4,889.00 €	1.55%	2,057.00 €	1.39
Bulgaria	2,192.00 €	1.08%	299.00 €	2,491.00 €	0.79%	1,893.00 €	1.61
Czech Republic	3,729.00 €	1.84%	1,887.00 €	5,616.00 €	1.78%	1,842.00 €	1.06
Poland	9,084.00 €	4.49%	3,596.00 €	12,680.00 €	4.01%	5,488.00 €	1.04
Greece	914.00 €	0.45%	234.00 €	1,148.00 €	0.36%	680.00 €	1.21
Turkey	7,290.20 €	3.60%	2,305.00 €	9,595.20 €	3.04%	4,985.20 €	1.12
Romania	1,502.00 €	0.74%	515.00 €	2,017.00 €	0.64%	987.00 €	0.88
Germany	23,655.00 €	11.70%	20,452.00 €	44,107.00 €	13.96%	3,203.00 €	0.18
Slovenia	209.00 €	0.10%	682.00 €	891.00 €	0.28%	-473.00 €	0.38
Italy	12,116.00 €	5.99%	6,480.00 €	18,596.00 €	5.88%	5,636.00 €	0.51
France	9,043.00 €	4.47%	5,009.00 €	14,052.00 €	4.45%	4,034.00 €	0.44
Belgium	3,965.00 €	1.96%	2,231.00 €	6,196.00 €	1.96%	1,734.00 €	0.31
SOURCE:					DG Trade & EUROSTAT		

Table 1-1. NATO Member States in Continental Europe Plus Ukraine: Trade with Russia Statistics (2009 Estimate). Continued.

Source: Enerdata, CIA Factbook, Gazprom Export LLC, DG Trade; and Eurostat energy statistics; author's calculations.

ENDNOTES - CHAPTER 1

1. Dick Lugar, "Senator Lugar's Keynote Speech to the German Marshall Fund Conference in Advance of the NATO Summit," Riga, Latvia, November 27, 2006.

2. In this monograph, the contemporary security environment refers to the way war is fought in the post-Cold War (or postmodern) environment, where the utility of force is diminishing, and diplomacy, information, and economics become methods of war just as relevant as, if not more important than, brute military force.

3. In a 2006 article, James Williams wrote that the "people's need for energy is essential for survival, so it is not surprising that energy production and consumption are some of the most important activities of human life. Indeed, it has been argued that energy is the key 'to the advance of civilization,' that the evolution of human societies is dependent on the conversion of energy for human use." See "Scientists and the Franklin Institute Making Their Cases," April 25, 2006, available from *www.fi.edu/learn/case-files/energy.html*.

4. In this monograph, the traditional security environment refers to the conceptualization of war as interstate conventional confrontations in which the utility of force (the notions of brute force, coercion, compellence, and deterrence) determines the way we look at strategic security concerns.

5. Bob Vavra, "1973: The Arab Oil Embargo Transforms the World," *National Petroleum News*, Vol. 92, No. 12, November 2000, p. 2.

6. Steve Chan and Cooper Drury, "Sanctions as Economic Statecraft: An Overview," Steve Chan and Cooper Drury, eds., *Sanctions as Economic Statecraft*, New York: St. Martin's Press, 2000, p. 1.

7. Dr. Bernard Cole, author of *The Great Wall at Sea* and professor at the National War College, is counted among the skeptics. Dr. Cole does not consider Russia as an "emerging power" in the energy field, mainly because Russia's economy is "rife with cor-

ruption, absence of rule of law (in the western sense), and lack of energy flexibility [and] over-dependence on energy resources." Bernard Cole, Interview by the author on Russia as an Energy Superstate, March 11, 2011.

This thesis will show that while Dr. Cole is right to consider China and India noteworthy energy security challengers of the United States because of their increasing demand for energy resources and the competition they will pose globally to acquire them, Russia remains very much a major energy security concern for many U.S. allies and NATO members in Eastern and Central Europe.

8. James Ngobi, "The United Nations Experience with Sanctions," George Lopez and David Cortright, eds., *Economic Sanctions. Panacea or Peacebuilding in a Post-Cold War World?* Boulder, CO: Westview Press, 1995, p. 19.

9. Chan and Drury, p. 2.

10. Ivan Eland, "Economic Sanctions as Tools of Foreign Policy," in Lopez and Cortright, p. 37.

11. Edward D. Mansfield, "Alliances, Preferential Trading Arrangements and Sanctions," *Journal of International Affairs*, Vol. 48, No. 1, Summer, 1994, p. 119.

12. Johan Galtung, "On the Effects of International Economic Sanctions: With Examples from the Case of Rhodesia." *World Politics*, Vol. 19, No. 3, April, 1967, pp. 378-416.

13. George Doran, *The Futility of Economic Sanctions as an Instrument of National Power in the 21st Century*, Carlisle, PA: U.S. Army War College, 1998.

14. Brendan Taylor, *Sanctions as Grand Strategy*, New York: The International Institute for Strategic Studies, 2010, p. 21.

15. David Mitrany, *The Problem of International Sanctions*, London, UK: Oxford University Press, 1925.

16. Chan and Drury, p. 1.

17. Gary C. Hufbauer, Jeffrey J. Schott, and Kimberly A. Elliott, eds., *Economic Sanctions Reconsidered. History and Current Policy*, Second Ed., Washington, DC: Institute for International Economics, 1990.

18. Claude E. Barfield and Mark A. Groombridge, "Unilateral Sanctions Undermine U.S. Interests," *The World and I*, December 1, 1998.

19. Nevin A. Bapat and T. Clifton Morgan, "Multilateral Versus Unilateral Sanctions Reconsidered: A Test Using New Data," *International Studies Quaterly*, Vol. 53, No. 1, December 2009, pp. 1075–1094.

20. Ralph Nurnberger, "Why Sanctions (almost) Never Work," *The International Economy*, Vol. 17, No. 4, Fall, 2003, p. 71.

21. Hossein G. Askari *et al.*, *Economic Sanctions. Examining their Philosophy and Efficacy*, Westport, CT: Praeger, 2003, p. 28.

22. David A. Baldwin, *Economic Statecraft*, Princeton, NJ: Princeton University Press, 1985, p. 65.

23. Chan and Drury, p. 2.

24. Hufbauer, Schott, and Elliott, p. 35.

25. *Ibid.*, p. 36.

26. Maria Sperandei, "Between Rational Choice and Historical Contingency: The Hidden Dilemma of Multiple Objectives in the Study of Economic Sanctions," *Conference Papers--International Studies Association*, 2009, pp. 1-34.

27. Ignoring the fact that some states are simply unwilling to share in the costs of sanctions, and will support them only if they get a free ride.

28. Sir Winston Churchill, as quoted in Shlomo Maital, "What We Can Offer Russia," *The Jerusalem Report*, October 22, 1992, p. 56.

29. Hufbauer, Schott, and Elliott, p. 48.

30. Bapat and Morgan, pp. 1075–1094.

31. Navin A. Bapat states that "although policymakers adamantly argue that multilateral sanctions are more effective than unilateral sanctions, the empirical evidence to date clearly suggests otherwise. Repeatedly, empirical studies demonstrate that [under certain political and economic conditions] unilateral sanctions appear more effective than multilateral sanctions." Bapat and Morgan, pp. 1075–1094.

32. Hufbauer, Schott, and Elliott.

33. T. Clifton Morgan, Navin Bapat, and Valentin Krustev, "The Threat and Imposition of Economic Sanctions, 1971-2000," *Conflict Management and Peace Science*, Vol. 26, No. 1, February, 2009, pp. 92-110.

34. Bapat and Morgan, pp. 1075–1094.

35. While the 1973 Arab Oil Embargo had economic repercussions, it did not accomplish its political ends, because of the lack of agreement among the sender states.

36. Alan Hegburg, "Keynote Speech on the Impact of Fossil Fuels on Security," Raleigh, NC: Triangle Institute for Security Studies, March 3, 2011.

37. Rosemary Kelanic, "Comments on the Impact of Fossil Fuels on Security," Raleigh, NC: Triangle Institute for Security Studies, March 3, 2011.

38. Dr. Rosemary Kelanic, an International Security Program Research Fellow at the Belfer Center for Science and International Affairs at Harvard University, recently designed and taught an advanced undergraduate course on oil and international security aimed at determining whether states can blackmail adversaries by threatening to cut off their access to oil, and if so, why. Her Ph.D. dissertation also examines the coercive potential of oil.

39. Roger Stern argued that "the oil weapon seems an implausible threat when the economic, geographic, and military attributes of prospective user and victim are considered." Roger

Stern, "Oil Market Power and United States National Security," *Proceedings of the National Academy of Sciences of the United States of America*, Vol. 103, No. 5, January 31, 2006, p. 1655.

40. Rosemary Kelanic, Alexander Ghaleb, "The Coercive Potential of Oil," Interview by the author conducted after the Energy and Security Initiative Conference 2011a, March 3, 2011.

41. Edward Harry Shaffer, "Canada's Oil and Imperialism," *International Journal of Political Economy*, Vol. 35, No. 2, Summer 2006, p. 55.

42. Keir Thorpe, "The Forgotten Shortage: Britain's Handling of the 1967 Oil Embargo," *Contemporary British History*, Vol. 21, No. 2, June 2007, p. 204.

43. *Ibid.*, p. 215.

44. Stern, p. 1650.

45. The oil embargo, however, failed to achieve its political objective, as Japan attacked Pearl Harbor instead of giving up its expansionist ideology. *Ibid.*

46. The recording was aired by the Finnish Broadcasting Company and presents a 1942 private conversation between Adolf Hitler and Finnish military commander Marshal Baron Carl Gustav Mannerheim. Toward the end of the recording, Hitler emphasized the importance of the Romanian oil supplies for the war efforts, and justified his preemptive advance Eastward by stating that his greatest concern from the very beginning was an invasion of Romania by the USSR. Hitler argued that "if the Russians had occupied Romania in the autumn of 1940 and acquired the petrol sources, then Germany would have been helpless in the year 1941 . . . without the addition of at least four or five million tons of Romanian oil, we wouldn't have been able to fight this war." Adolf Hitler, *Private Conversation between Adolf Hitler and the Finnish Military Commander, Marshal Baron Carl Gustav Mannerheim*, Adolf Hitler and Baron Carl Gustav Mannerheim, Recording, 1942 Finnish Broadcasting Company.

47. Mohammed Ahrari, "OAPEC and 'Authoritative' Allocation of Oil: An Analysis of the Arab Oil Embargo," *Studies in Comparative International Development*, Vol. 14, No. 1, Spring 1979, p. 13.

48. *Ibid.*, p. 16.

49. Stern, p. 1650.

50. Kelanic, "Comments on the Impact of Fossil Fuels on Security."

51. Dr. Kelanic argued that because the global market for oil is more flexible than that of natural gas, oil can be transported safely in mulitiple ways from mulitple places along different trade routes. In short, the global market for oil is much more flexible and adapts to changes in supply. No one state has full control over oil imports in relation to another state.

52. John Deutch argued that "since natural gas is cheaper than oil on an equivalent energy basis, meaning the price per BTU [British thermal unit] is lower, over time natural gas will begin to replace oil, first in the power sector and then in the industrial and transportation sectors." John Deutch, "The Good News about Gas: The Natural Gas Revolution and its Consequences," *Foreign Affairs*, Vol. 90, No. 1, January 2011, p. 89.

53. Joe Barnes *et al.*, "Introduction to the Study," David G. Victor, Amy M. Jaffe, and Mark H. Hayes, eds., *Natural Gas and Geopolitics from 1970 to 2040*, New York: Cambridge University Press, 2006, p. 21. Also, Amy M. Jaffe, Mark H. Hayes, and David G. Victor, "Gas Geopolitics: Visions to 2040," Program on Energy and Sustainable Development, PESD. Working Paper #36, *Natural Gas and Geopolitics: From 1970 to 2040*, Stanford, CA: Institute for International Studies, 2005.

54. Rita Tubb, "Study Finds Nation's Natural Gas Supply Will Last Well into Next Century," *Pipeline & Gas Journal*, Vol. 237, No. 4, April, 2010, pp. 34-36.

55. David Wagman, "Natural Gas Rising," *Power Engineering*, Vol. 114, No. 10, October 2010, p. 6.

56. "Natural Gas' Path to Low-Carbon Future," *USA Today Magazine*, Vol. 139, No. 2782, July, 2010, p. 7.

57. Roberto F. Aguilera, "The Future of the European Natural Gas Market: A Quantitative Assessment," *Energy*, Vol. 35, No. 8, August, 2010, pp. 3332-3339.

58. "INGAA Responds to Report on Reliance of Natural Gas for Electricity," *Underground Construction*, Vol. 65, No. 9, September, 2010, p. 8.

59. Barnes *et al.*, p. 3. Also see Deutch, p. A17; and Jaffe, Hayes, and Victor.

60. Barnes *et al.*, p. 3.

61. *Ibid*.

62. Matthew L. Wald, "Study Says Natural Gas Use Likely to Double," *New York Times*, June 25, 2010, p. 3.

63. Carlos Márquez and Gina M. Hernández, "Natural Gas: The Cleanest Fossil Fuel Catches on," *Caribbean Business*, Vol. 38, No. 15, April 22, 2010, p. 27. Also see Deutch, p. A17.

64. Barnes *et al.*, p. 21.

65. "Congress Should Do More to Support Natural Gas as Fuel: NGVAmerica Chief," *Bulk Transporter*, Vol. 72, No. 12, June, 2010, p. 12-12; Christine Birkner, "Natural Gas in a Range," *Futures: News, Analysis & Strategies for Futures, Options & Derivatives Traders*, Vol. 39, No. 4, April, 2010, p. 16.

66. Wald, p. 3.

67. Carlos Márquez and Gina M. Hernández, "Everybody is on Board: Increased Use of Natural Gas Essential to Reduce Energy Costs in the Short Term," *Caribbean Business*, Vol. 38, No. 15, April 22, 2010, pp. 20-27.

68. Barnes *et al.*, p. 3; Rita Tubb, *Future Role of Natural Gas and Shale Revolution Dominate at P&GJ's 2010 Pipeline Opportunities*

Conference, Vol. 237, Houston, TX: Oildom Publishing Company of Texas, Inc, 2010, pp. 22-26.

69. "Uneven Prospects for Natural-Gas Vehicles," *Machine Design*, Vol. 82, No. 13, August 12, 2010, pp. 23-26; Márquez and Hernández, p. 27.

70. Barnes *et al.*, p. 3; *Natural Gas' Path to Low-Carbon Future*.

71. Márquez and Hernández, p. 27; Deutch, p. A17.

72. Nicholas Apergis and James E. Payne, "Natural Gas Consumption and Economic Growth: A Panel Investigation of 67 Countries," *Applied Energy*, Vol. 87, No. 8, August 2010, pp. 2759-2763.

73. Wagman, p. 6.

74. Birkner, p. 16.

75. Peter Huber, "Kill Oil with Natural Gas and Electricity: A Carbon Strategy the World can Afford," *Energy Policy & the Environment Report*, No. 4, September 2009.

76. *Ibid.*

77. This begs the question: If driving an NVG is cleaner and cheaper, why aren't they flooding the market? The problem lies in the lack of infrastructure and the high costs to install CNG (compressed natural gas) pumps. According to the Department of Energy datasets, California has the largest number of CNG pumps, with close to 300, followed by New York, with almost 200; while most states have 10 or fewer CNG pumps each, with South Dakota, Iowa, and Kentucky not having any CNG pumps available for customers at all. This data was calculated from "Natural Gas Fueling Station Locations," Washington, DC: Department of Energy, available from *www.afdc.energy.gov/afdc/fuels/natural_gas_locations.html*.

78. *Uneven Prospects for Natural-Gas Vehicles*, pp. 23-26.

79. Barnes *et al.*, p. 21.

80. Tubb, pp. 22-26.

81. Daniel Yergin is also the author of the 1992 Pulitzer Prize winner and number one bestseller, *The Prize: The Epic Quest for Oil, Money, and Power*. In 1997, Yergin was awarded the United States Energy Award for "lifelong achievements in energy and the promotion of international understanding."

82. Richard A. Kerr, "Natural Gas from Shale Bursts Onto the Scene," *Science*, Vol. 328, No. 5986, June 25, 2010, pp. 1624-1626.

83. Wagman, p. 6.

84. Deutch, p. A17.

85. Amy M. Jaffe and Ronald Soligo, "Market Structure in the New Gas Economy: Is Cartelization Possible?" David G. Victor, Amy M. Jaffe, and Mark H. Hayes, eds., *Natural Gas and Geopolitics from 1970 to 2040*, New York: Cambridge University Press, 2006, p. 445.

86. Liquefied Natural Gas (LNG) is widely considered a significant tool to diversify the supply of natural gas, and is a "decisive factor in developing a global gas market." Unlike pipelines, "the tanker-based LNG trade is much more flexible and does not lend itself as a geopolitical instrument." See Florian Baumann and Georg Simmerl, *Between Conflict and Convergence: The EU Member States and the Quest for a Common External Energy Policy*, Research Group on European Affairs, 2011, p. 29.

87. As Greenspan put it, "natural gas reserves are somewhat more widely dispersed than those of oil, for which three-fifths of proved world reserves reside in the Middle East. Nearly two-fifths of world natural gas reserves are in Russia and its former satellites, and one-third is in the Middle East."

88. Alan Greenspan. Committee on Energy and Commerce, U.S. House of Representatives, *Natural Gas Supply and Demand Issues*, 2003.

89. *Ibid.*

90. $6.31 per million Btu.

91. $3.65 per million Btu.

92. Daniel Freifeld argued that "unlike oil, which can be put onto tankers and shipped anywhere, gas is generally moved in pipelines that traverse, and are thus tethered to, geography. Because a pipeline cannot be rerouted . . . today's gas war is a zero-sum conflict similar to the scramble for resources that divided Eurasia in the 19th century." This was also underlined by Sergej Mahnovski, who wrote that "the most salient difference between oil and gas markets today is that gas markets are almost entirely regional, due to prohibitively high transportation costs. In fact, many energy analysts believe that approximately one-half of the natural gas reserves in the world are currently— 'stranded' economically or technically unfeasible to transport to existing markets with today's technologies. Abundant gas reserves in many parts of the world are either flared or reinjected into oil wells to boost reservoir pressure, rather than transported to markets, due to high capital costs associated with natural gas pipeline construction and operation." Daniel Freifeld, "The Great Pipeline Opera," *Foreign Policy*, No. 174, September, 2009, p. 123; Sergej Mahnovski, "Natural Resources and Potential Conflict in the Caspian Sea Region," Thomas Szayna, ed., *Fault-Lines of Conflict in Central Asia and the South Caucasus*, Santa Monica, CA: RAND, 2003, p. 115.

93. Greenspan.

94. Richard Newell, "Annual Energy Outlook 2011 Reference Case," Washington, DC: The Paul H. Nitze School of Advanced International Studies, December 16, 2010.

95. Don Maxwell and Zhen Zhu, "Natural Gas Prices, LNG Transport Costs, and the Dynamics of LNG Import," *Energy Economics*, Vol. 33, No. 2, March, 2011, pp. 217-226.

96. Julie A. Urban, "US Access to the Global LNG Market," *OPEC Energy Review*, Vol. 32, No. 3, September, 2008, p. 223.

97. *Ibid.*

98. *Ibid.*, p. 224.

99. Robert Cekuta, Deputy Assistant Secretary, Energy, Sanctions and Commodities at the Department of State, also acknowledged that cost is a prohibiting factor for many developing countries. This is not the case only with LNG terminals, but also with developing a natural gas pipeline infrastructure that is bi-directional (from West to East): "In building infrastructure, the first thought that comes to mind is cost--the companies need to see it as something on which it is worth spending the money. Building in the duplication needed for energy security is not cheap." Robert Cekuta, Interview by the author on the Cost of Natural Gas Infrastructure in Eurasia, March 12, 2011; *Flexibility in Natural Gas Supply and Demand*, Paris, France: OECD/IEA, 2002.

100. The difficulty in decreasing the dependence on natural gas imports by pipeline has also been emphasized by RAND Policy Expert Sergej Mahnovski, who wrote that "natural" gas pipeline transport involves a careful matching of forecasted supply and demand. Whereas crude oil and other liquid products can be transported by some combination of rail, truck, or ship without major processing, natural gas must be compressed, liquefied, or chemically transformed to take advantage of nonpipeline transport." Sergej Mahnovski, "Natural Resources and Potential Conflict in the Caspian Sea Region," in Szayna, ed., *Fault-Lines of Conflict in Central Asia and the South Caucasus*, p. 120.

101. Similarly with oil, Russia supplies over 85 percent of Bulgarian, Hungarian, and Polish oil imports. However, Daniel Drezner argued that target states that rely on the sender for more than 80 percent of their energy demands or 50 percent of their trade face significant costs as a result of coercion. For the reasons discussed above, Russia never used oil successfully as an instrument of coercion. Daniel Drezner, "The Complex Causation of Sanction Outcomes," in Chan and Drury, eds., *Sanctions as Economic Statecraft*, p. 224.

102. Urban, p. 228.

103. *Ibid.*, p. 222.

104. "Europe Boosts LNG Purchases," *Russia Beyond the Headlines*, June 10, 2010.

105. Jeffrey Mankoff, *Eurasian Energy Security*, Washington, DC: Council on Foreign Relations, 2009.

106. *Flexibility in Natural Gas Supply and Demand*, p. 45.

107. TPES refers to total primary energy supply, or the aggregate of all energy resources, such as oil, gas, coal, nuclear, hydro, and other renewables.

108. Keith Smith, *Russia-Europe Energy Relations. Implications for U.S. Policy*, Washington, DC: CSIS, 2010.

109. *Ibid.*

110. M. K. Amb Bhadrakumar, "Pipeline Geopolitics: Major Turnaround. Russia, China, Iran Redraw Energy Map. Turkmenistan Commits its Gas Exports to China, Russia & Iran." *Global Research*, January 12, 2010, October 27, 2010.

111. Nabucco is a U.S.-backed natural gas pipeline from Azerbaijan to Austria meant to diversify the supply of natural gas to Europe.

112. Rolan Lajtai, Annamária Czinkos, and Tamás Dinh, "NABUCCO VS. SOUTH STREAM: The Effects and Feasibility in the Central and Eastern European Region," 24th World Gas Conference, Buenos Aires, Argentina, KPMG in Central and Eastern Europe, October 5-9, 2009.

113. Urban, p. 228.

114. According to RePEc (Research Papers in Economics), Andrei Shleifer is the most cited economist in the world. He is also one of the engineers of the Russian privatization of the 1990s.

115. Professor Daniel Treisman also has experience with a U.S. Agency for International Development (USAID) team advising Russia's finance ministry on tax reform in the 1990s.

116. Andrei Shleifer and Daniel Treisman, "Why Moscow Says No: A Question of Russian Interests, Not Psychology," *Foreign Affairs*, Vol. 90, No. 1, January 2011, p. 129.

117. *Ibid.*, p. 128.

118. *Ibid.*, p. 126.

119. *Ibid.*, p. 128.

120. *Ibid.*

121. Deutch, p. 89.

122. Kerr, pp. 1624-1626.

123. Barnes *et al.*, p. 22.

124. Birkner, p. 16.

125. A report published in February 2011 by the Center for Applied Policy Research writes that this common energy policy

> is seriously hampered by member states' efforts to defend their sovereignty: based on differing energy mixes, differing suppliers, and differing priorities the member states pursue national energy strategies that are only barely compatible with each other. Despite a perceived similarity of the challenges the member states face and the strategic objectives they ascribe to a common energy policy, security of supply, stable prices, and environmental protection, they nevertheless adhere to national strategies, which make them pull the common energy policy into opposite directions.

Florian Baumann and Georg Simmerl, *Between Conflict and Convergence: The EU Member States and the Quest for a Common External Energy Policy*, Research Group on European Affairs, 2011, p. 2.

126. Figure 1-3 accurately indicates the degree of asymmetry in diversification of natural gas trade partners, especially between ECE countries and Russia.

127. *Ibid.*, p. 87.

128. *Europe Boosts LNG Purchases.*

129. "Swinoujscie LNG Gas Terminal, Baltic Coast, Poland," *Hydrocarbons Technology,* available from *www.hydrocarbons-technology.com/projects/swinoujscie.*

130. "Azerbaijan-Romania LNG Project may Cost 4.5bn Euros," *News.Az,* February 15, 2011.

131. Shale gas deposits refers to tight gas, which is found in relatively impermeable rock formations.

132. Deutch, *The Good News about Gas,* p. 86.

133. *Ibid.*

134. *Ibid.*

135. These conclusions have also been reinforced by RAND's Sergej Mahnovski, who argued that:

> although they face similar obstacles, such as low domestic demand and high transportation costs to foreign markets, crude oil and natural gas producers must consider fundamentally different transportation options. With the exception of large markets with overland routes, potential crude oil pipeline expansions would likely terminate at high-capacity ports with access to international waterways in the Black Sea, Persian Gulf, Mediterranean Sea, and possibly the Indian Ocean. In contrast, natural gas pipelines would lead directly to regional hubs near demand centers, since large-scale maritime transport is impossible without capital-intensive liquefaction plants.

Mahnovski, "Natural Resources and Potential Conflict in the Caspian Sea Region," p. 115.

136. Kathleen Davis, "EU Energy Commissioner Gets on 2020 Bandwagon," *POWERGRID International,* Vol. 15, No. 12, December 2010, p. 12.

137. This figure tells us that in Lithuania, for example, natural gas occupies 31.6 percent of the sum of all energy resources in that country, all of which is being supplied by Russia. The higher the share of TPES representing Russian natural gas, the more that country depends on Russian gas. It must be noted that 10 percent of TPES representing Russian natural gas is considered extremely high, and reflects on the country's failure to diversify its energy supply.

138. It is important to look at the trade deficit with Russia because it significantly increases the costs of coercion when sanctions are imposed by Russia. Figure 1-6 underlines that even if 57 percent of Russia world trade comes from the European Union (EU), half of that is coming from trade with Europe's center (Germany, Italy, and France) alone. Furthermore, in 2009 EU had a near 50-billion euro trade deficit with Russia; with only 12 billion being attributed to Europe's center, while the rest of the deficit is attributed mostly to Europe's periphery, ECE countries.

139. "Lithuania Demands Fair Gas Price from Gazprom." *Reuters*, March 3, 2011.

140. "Lithuania Demands Fair Price from Gazprom," *The Baltic Times*, March 4, 2011.

141. Mankoff, p. 33.

142. To better understand how this susceptibility to Russian coercion works, let us consider the economic effects on Bulgaria, which ranks as the second most susceptible country to Russian coercion, in case Russia were to cut its natural gas supplies. I chose Bulgaria to focus on because data are readily available—during the January 2009 gas supply cut to Ukraine, Bulgaria's natural gas shortfall was 100 percent for 14 days—making it easier to estimate the economic effects if Russia were to cut its natural gas supplies to Bulgaria alone in the future. Edward Christie, Research Partner with the Pan-European Institute (PEI) of the Turku School of Economics, Finland, estimated that Bulgaria suffered significant economic losses during this period: "[I]ndustrial production fell, in seasonally-adjusted terms, in line with the share of natural gas in the energy product mix in Bulgarian industry, namely 23 percent for the 14-day period of the cut. The economy-wide effect

may have been in the order of 0.35 percent of yearly gross domestic product (GDP), corresponding to a 9.1 percent GDP shortfall for the 14-day period of the cut." This was also confirmed by the Bulgarian government, which estimated the cost to the Bulgarian economy at 250-million euros (for the duration of the 14 days), indicating that in the future, if Russia were to cut its natural gas to Bulgaria, the Bulgarian economy would collapse in a matter of months. Edward Christie, Pavel Baev, and Volodymyr Golovko, "Vulnerability and Bargaining Power in EU-Russia Gas Relations," *FIW-Research Reports 2010/11*, No. 3, March, 2011, p. 1.

CHAPTER 2

THE SALIENCE OF NATURAL GAS
IN THE EMERGING GEOPOLITICAL MODEL
OF RUSSIA
AS AN ENERGY SUPERSTATE

The gas pipeline system is the creation of the Soviet Union.[1]

Vladimir Putin

Winston Churchill once admitted that he could not forecast "the action of Russia. It is a riddle wrapped in a mystery inside an enigma."[2] What is clear today, however, is that Russia is on a quest to achieve the status of a great power—a quest that is promoted not only by Prime Minister Vladimir Putin, but by most of Russia's political class—and it perceives the North Atlantic Treaty Organization (NATO) as a hostile alliance that is meddling in its backyard (rather than as a prospective ally).[3] This fact is important to bear in mind, because it provides a strong argument that Russia will use natural gas as an instrument of coercion against the European Union (EU) and NATO member states most susceptible to this type of coercion—particularly those listed in Figure 1-4: Lithuania, Bulgaria, Croatia, Slovakia, Hungary, Latvia, Greece, and Estonia—just as it has in Ukraine—a case that this monograph will analyze in the next chapter. Russia will do this in order to influence the decisionmaking processes of these nations—a strategy that will be discussed later in the monograph.

Putin's Russia understands that it does not have the means to confront NATO militarily, but that it stands a chance to achieve its grand strategic objectives only by using its vast natural resources, like oil and natural gas. This chapter makes a case that Russia's status as a world power cannot be achieved without the use of oil to increase Russia's national wealth, and without the use of natural gas to promote Russia's national interests in a well-defined sphere of influence. While only natural gas can be used successfully as an instrument of coercion—as discussed in Chapter 1—oil remains an important piece of the puzzle, because it provides Russia the profits it needs not only to grow its economy, but also to leverage the losses incurred from Russia's use of natural gas primarily for political rather than economic ends.[4] But while much has been written about Russia's use of oil to amass great wealth, little has been written about Russia's use of natural gas as an instrument of state power—despite the fact that this detail stands out when analyzing the Energy Strategy of Russia through 2030, the Foreign Policy Concept, and the National Security Strategy (NSS) of the Russian Federation until 2020.

RUSSIA'S FOREIGN POLICY . . . IS THE COLD WAR OVER?

Over the past decade, a series of overlooked but obvious developments in the Eastern part of the EU— to include an increase in the demand for Russian natural gas—contributed to the "emergence of a more confident and assertive Russia"[5] that threatens not only the stability and security of the European continent, but also the unity and the very indissolubility of the Euro-Atlantic sphere. As Frederic Labarre from the Partnership for Peace Consortium put it, "Russia is back," and is on the verge "of becoming the new hegemon in Eastern and Central Europe [ECE],[6] an area intersecting with the interests of EU and NATO member states. The macro-strategic postulate is that a new world order is dawning before us."[7]

To appease these concerns, the 2010 Institute of Contemporary Development (INSOR[8]) report, *Russia of the Twenty-First Century: The Image of the Desired Future*, argues that Russia is not a threat to the West, among others reasons, because Russia's impending foreign policy goals include membership in both the EU and NATO.[9] To date, however, Russia has not shown any indication of its intent to join the former, and has repeatedly shown contempt toward the latter.

Because geographically half of Russia is in Europe, some security analysts mistakably assume that Russia is a European nation, and thus its interests ought to coincide with those of the West. In contrast to geography, however, political influences are not so axiomatic,[10] and the past century of Russian history illustrates that Russia will resist any Western agenda of democratization.[11] The bigger half of the Russian territory lies east of the Urals, on the Asian continent, whose outlook on life and the management of society plays an equally important role in defining Russia's foreign and domestic policy. This aspect was emphasized by Russian Foreign Minister Andrei Kozyrev during a 1992 speech before the Conference on Security and Cooperation in Europe (CSCE):

> We realize that our traditions come mostly, if not altogether, from Asia, which establishes certain limits on the rapprochement with Western Europe. . . . The territory of the former Soviet Union cannot be regarded as the zone of full application of CSCE norms. In fact, this is post-imperial territory where Russia will have to defend its interests by using all available means, including military and economic ones.[12]

The resistance to Western thought was also emphasized by Putin, who argued in 2007 — while he was still the President of the Russian Federation — that "blindly copying foreign models, will inevitably lead to Russia losing its national identity."[13] To this effect, Jerrold Schecter — former *Time* magazine's Moscow bureau chief, and a former member of the National Security Council — argued that Russian national identity is "fueled chiefly by two forces: one is practical interest; the other, equally potent, is Russian nationalism."[14]

The practical interest in the post-Cold War Russia has undergone a series of "cognitive processes"[15] that separated it over the past 2 decades from the Marxist-Leninist ideology of the communist period. Ian Bremmer — president and founder of Eurasia Group — wrote that Post-Soviet Russia follows a pragmatic approach in its relations with the West where practical interest presides over the notion of partnership: "When Moscow finally decided to welcome the increasingly free flow of ideas, information, people, money, goods, and services from beyond their borders, they would try their best to control these processes, and to carefully micromanage the risks they create."[16] This cautious approach to foreign policy became much more obvious after Putin became president and as he promoted change in a more "piecemeal fashion" than his predecessor.[17]

Russian unconventional wisdom under Putin was supplemented by Putin's neo-Soviet/nationalist nostalgia, in itself defined in restorationist terms. Putin consolidated his power by promoting the organic unity of Russia as "distinct from both European and Asian cultures,"[18] and by advocating for geopolitical expansion as proven by "constant and explicit references to the glorious Soviet past,"[19] and by his viewpoint on the collapse of the Soviet Union as the "greatest catastrophe of the 20th century."[20] As Alexandre Mansourov—Senior Associate of the Nautilus Institute for Security and Sustainable Development—put it, "empire-building based on national consolidation and external expansion is the most popular theme of public discourse, a magnet for elite opinions, and an integral part of President Putin's modernization project."[21] The problem is that this preoccupation with achieving imperial self-sufficiency through the restoration of "Russia's geopolitical status as the Eurasian Heartland" is not characteristic only to Putin, but to almost the entire Russian political class.[22] Anatoly Chubais—former First Deputy Prime Minister of Russia—envisions a "Liberal empire"; ultra-nationalist Alexander Prokhanov—a "White empire"; Gennady Yuganov—First Secretary of the Communist Party of the Russian Federation—a "Red empire"; Aleksandr Dugin—president of the Eurasia Party—a "Eurasian empire"; Dmitry Olegovich Rogozin—Ambassador Extraordinary and Plenipotentiary of Russia to NATO—a "Patriotic empire"; Eduard Limonov—leader of the radical National Bolshevik Party—a "National-Bolshevik empire"; and finally, Vladimir Zhirinovsky—Vice Chairman of the State Duma and leader of the Liberal Democratic Party of Russia—an "All-Russian Empire."[23]

Envisioning a Russia free of any Euro-Atlantic influences,[24] Putin stated in his 2007 speech at the Munich Conference on Security Policy that Russia "will no longer accept the status of the West's junior partner as during the 1990s";[25] sending a clear message to the West that Russia's interests are unlikely to overlap those of the Euro-Atlantic community in the near future.[26] This antagonistic relationship between Russia and the West was further affected by the NATO enlargement eastward, which was largely perceived not only as a threat to "Russia's international status and role,"[27] but as a betrayal by the North Atlantic Alliance.

Russia's bitter reaction to the decision to base NATO antimissile facilities in Eastern and Central European countries—particularly in Poland and the Czech Republic—further shows that Russia regards NATO as a hostile alliance, more than as a prospective ally.[28] This comes, however, as no surprise. From the very beginning, Russia viewed the eastward expansion of the North Atlantic Alliance as a direct provocation that challenged Russia's security interests abroad.[29] According to the Russian leadership, the Alliance was meddling in "Russia's backyard,"[30] and even though Russia lacked the power to prevent the expansion, its leaders threatened countermeasures if the West ignored the Kremlin.[31] As indicated in 1992 by former Russian Defense Minister Igor Rodionov, Russia insisted on the following points after the fall of the Soviet Union:

> The neutrality of East-European countries or their friendly relations with Russia; free Russian access to seaports in the Baltics; the exclusion of "third country" military forces from the Baltics and non-membership of the Baltic states in military blocks directed at Russia; the prevention of the countries that constitute the CIS [Commonwealth of Independent States] from becoming part of a buffer zone aimed at separating Russia from the West, South, or East; maintaining the CIS states under Russia's exclusive influence.[32]

Former Russian Defense Minister Sergei Ivanov also insisted (this time in 2004) that it made no sense for NATO to expand eastward because the countries bordering Russia – particularly the Baltic states – were "consumers, not producers of collective security in the region."[33] The Russian leadership also argued that Russia is better posed to provide security for its neighbors, and has even voiced its willingness to guarantee their territorial integrity and independence. These promises were met, however, with contempt by Russia's former allies, and, as Latvian President Guntis Ulmanis put it, any alliance between the Baltic States and Russia was viewed as "the second annexation of the Baltic by Russia."[34]

In the end, seven former Warsaw Pact members – Bulgaria, Hungary, Poland, Romania, Slovenia, the Czech Republic, and Slovakia – and three "ex-Soviet republics"[35] – Estonia, Latvia, and Lithuania – were invited to join the Alliance.[36] Russia viewed this as a violation of an alleged 1989 no-NATO-enlargement pledge made to Soviet President Mikhail Gorbachev in exchange for allowing the German reunification.[37]

According to Minton Goldman, a Professor Emeritus of Comparative Politics at Northeastern University who holds a Ph.D. from the Fletcher School of Law and Diplomacy, the NATO eastward expansion ushered in ". . . a new phase of competition and confrontation between Russia and the West."[38] This appraisal transcends all levels of Russian social strata. According to a 2011 opinion poll by the Russian *Analytical Digest*, the top five enemies of Russia – in this order – are Chechen gunmen (48 percent of Russians believe Chechen gunmen are enemies of Russia); the United States (40 percent); NATO (32 percent); other political forces in the West (30 percent); and Islamic fundamentalism (27 percent).[39] International editor of *The Economist* Edward Lucas also agreed with Goldman's assessment, adding, however, that Russia "lacks the Soviet Union's hard power-military muscle, and seems unable to find a rival to Euroatlanticism."[40]

While Russia's interests are unlikely to overlap those of the Euro-Atlantic community in the next couple of decades, it is also unlikely that Russia will have the means to confront the West militarily.[41] In his Ph.D. dissertation, however, Putin was less concerned about the state of the Russian military, and emphasized instead the strategic potential of the vast regional natural resources as Russia's main source of state power.

In 1904, Sir Halford John Mackinder (English geographer, considered by many the founding father of geostrategy) warned that Russia could replace the Mongol Empire as the largest contiguous empire in history, because it occupies in the world at large "the central strategical position held by Germany in Europe."[42] This world empire, he argued, will be in sight if Russia exploits its "vast continental resources."[43] Some energy security professionals believe that Mackinder's point was also underlined by Putin in his Ph.D. in Economics dissertation from the Saint Petersburg State Mining University. After reading Putin's dissertation, Dr. Christina Lin, former director for policy planning at the United States Department of Defense, described the document as Putin's plan to use the Russian resource sector to "once again reassert Russia's imperial status."[44]

While natural gas did not play a significant role in Putin's manuscript, the strategic planning and the management by the state of the production and transportation of natural resources did.[45] In the introduction, Russia is presented as a "region with high natural resource and industrial-economic potential." Putin then writes that the purpose of his study is the "strategic planning of natural resources in the region, including the formation of national strategy, forecasting, and planning of national strategic goals and objectives, as well as economic incentives, levers, and incentives for implementation of the strategy [by the state]." This "geo-economic," "long-term" planning of natural resources by the state, he argued, "is applicable to solving any problem associated with national objectives abroad . . . and for the regional organization of export-oriented natural resources industries."[46] Ian Bremmer argued that the application of these principles during his time as the President of the Russian Federation, between 2000 and 2008, labels Putin as the chief architect of state capitalism in Russia and a strong promoter of resource nationalism[47] as the driving force behind Russia's current economic and political structure.[48]

Bremmer defined state capitalism—not to be confused with the traditional Soviet social central planning—as a form of a bureaucratically engineered capitalism "in which the state plays the role of the leading economic actor and uses markets primarily for political gain."[49] Like mercantilism, state capitalism is a form of economic nationalism "for the purpose of building a wealthy and powerful state; . . . it is an economic system in which governments use state regulation to amass national wealth and power at the expense of all other governments,"[50] even at the expense of the free market:

> As with mercantilism, state capitalists use markets to build state power. Forced to choose between protection of the rights of the individual, economic productivity, and the principle of consumer choice, on the one hand, and the achievement of political goals, on the other, state capitalists would choose the latter every time.[51]

Like the mercantilist merchants, contemporary state capitalists—such as Vladimir Putin—consider themselves "warriors on the front lines of a great national effort"[52] to increase the national wealth and to promote the national interests and the nation's status as a world power; not at the expense of crown colonies, but at the expense of a well-defined sphere of influence:

> State capitalists see markets primarily as a tool that serves national interests, or at least those of ruling elites, rather than as an engine of opportunity for the individual. State capitalists use markets to extend their own political and economic leverage—both within society and on the international stage. State capitalism is not an ideology. It's not simply Communism by another name or an updated form of central planning. It embraces capitalism, but for its own purposes.[53]

But state capitalism in Russia is not 21st-century mercantilism; nor is it a revamped version of socialism. Ernest Raiklin, a Professor of Economics at the University of Northern Iowa who previously taught economics in St. Petersburg, Russia, predicted the advent of Russian state capitalism as early as 1989, defining it as a form of "authoritarian mixed capitalism," which combines central strategic planning and the lack of political democracy with Western capitalism.[54] Today, both Putin, and Dimitri Medvedev see world trade with positive eyes. With regard to mercantilism, President Medvedev vowed that Russia "will not repeat the historic mistakes of protectionism of previous eras."[55] Furthermore, talking about command economics, Putin previously stated that "any Russian who doesn't regret the disintegration of the Soviet

Union has no heart, but one who wants to revive it has no head."[56] In his dissertation and during his years in power, Putin has "repeatedly affirmed his conviction that only capitalism—in this case, state capitalism—can generate prosperity in Russia and restore the country to great-power status."[57]

On the Eurasian plateau, the power of the Kremlin is back; primarily because of Russia's vast natural resources, like oil and gas—exactly as both Mackinder and Putin predicted would happen. This use of natural resources by the state as geo-strategic tools is also known as resource nationalism.

Effectively linked to the function of the Kremlin in the operation and strategic management of the energy industry,[58] Russian resource nationalism is a type of "post-Soviet Russian-style laissez-faire capitalism"[59] that is best described as a "blood sport"[60] with referees who represent the interests of the state, of the political elite, and of Putin's oligarchs—dubbed as patriots—to the detriment of everyone else. To this effect, Bremmer wrote that "nowhere is resource nationalism played on a grander scale than in Russia."[61] Over the past decade, Russia has been consolidating its control over the energy sector through the use of "national champions"[62] closely aligned with the Kremlin—such as state monopolies, Transneft and Gazprom—where the government maintains ownership of more than 50-percent equity,[63] thus effectively containing the power held by foreign investors in the oil and gas industries.[64]

Through the use of resource nationalism, Russia effectively managed to become an "energy superstate,"[65] a geo-political model that allows Russia to use its natural resources—and in particular its natural gas reserves—as strategic assets and political tools in its foreign relations and negotiations with many European and NATO countries.[66] The main benefactors of this energy superstate—Russia's political elite—understand that the control of the natural gas pipeline networks is a matter of geopolitics, just as oil was while still remaining to a certain extent a matter of economics.[67] Both the political—promoted through the use of natural gas reserves—and the economic rationality[68] are meant, however, to act as tools to project Russian power abroad.[69]

Russia leverages its natural resources and energy sector—including the natural gas pipeline networks—to achieve both domestic political stability and geopolitical objectives.[70] Domestically, the Russian political elite uses the large revenues it generates from exporting its natural gas resources to accomplish political goals.[71] Furthermore, by securing its control of the production and transportation networks of natural gas, the political elite has been able to effectively take control of all major centers of political power.[72] Internationally, Russia is actively using its natural gas production and transportation systems "as weapons with which to reestablish dominance throughout the territory of the former Soviet Union,"[73] and to reassert its primacy "over both the energy-producing states of Central Asia and the energy consuming states of Europe."[74] In each case, Bremmer wrote, "the primary motive is political."[75]

Sustainment of this geopolitical model, however, depends on revenues from oil production and on maintaining a monopoly on the sphere of natural gas production and transportation West of the Urals.[76] On the former, Russia's economic development depends on large profits from oil; and on the latter, exerting political influence in many Eastern and Central Europe

(ECE) countries depends on maintaining a monopoly on natural gas transportation infrastructure.

Paul Domjan — who previously served as the first energy security advisor to the United States European Command (EUCOM) and is currently an energy fellow at the Stockholm Network — rightly characterized resource nationalism as "a wide range of strategies that domestic elites employ in order to increase their control of natural resources" for political and economic gain.[77] As we have seen above, resource nationalism in Russia is "a matter of the government's political survival,"[78] and acts as a politico-economic tool to facilitate the control of the periphery by the center — both within Russia and in its sphere of influence:[79]

> Domestic stability is served by ensuring that "the commanding heights" of the economy — in this case, the energy sector — do not generate centers of political power outside the purview of the central government. Geopolitical influence is served by controlling the majority of Eurasian gas and oil export pipelines, enabling the Russian government simultaneously to exert influence over Central Asian energy producers and European energy consumers. [80]

Because the economic objectives of the oil sector and the geostrategic objectives of the gas sector are "subordinate to political goals that are designed to reassert the primacy of the state in domestic and foreign affairs,"[81] resource nationalism can only be supported by a "strategic long-term policy choice."[82] This point has also been argued by Putin earlier in the chapter — particularly in his thesis — who also views Russia's natural resources as ideal geopolitical tools "to reinstate Russia as a great power in a multi-polar world order."[83] Furthermore, resource nationalism also became an integral part of Russia's NSS.

RUSSIA'S GEO-ECONOMIC REALISM: THE NATIONAL SECURITY STRATEGY AND NATURAL GAS

The theory that the current NSS is, in fact, an extension of Putin's economics dissertation is not at all far-fetched. Written by a committed state capitalist, Putin's dissertation comes with one clear-cut message: that "the management of Russia's natural resources is too important to leave to private business."[84] As the chief originator of post-Soviet resource nationalism, Putin views the energy sector — and particularly natural gas — as an effective tool that Russia can use to regain its strength — as he put it in his 2006 State of the Nation Address — because "the weak get beaten."[85]

Russia is the world's leading natural gas producer and exporter,[86] and controls almost a quarter of the natural gas trade worldwide.[87] Because of this, Russia's geopolitical and energy potential lies in its natural gas reserves and export pipeline networks. Not surprisingly, at a 2005 meeting of the Russian Security Council and at the 2006 Saint-Petersburg G8 Summit, President Putin's speeches "gave rise to discussion of a new foreign policy idea — Russia as an energy superstate."[88] David Ignatius, co-author of *America and the World: Conversations on the Future of American Foreign Policy*, asserted that Moscow is "on its way to becoming the next Houston — the global capital of energy."[89] Peter Rutland, former visiting Fulbright professor at the European University in St. Petersburg, disagreed with this contention, arguing that Russia cannot use oil and natural gas as weapons because "the global energy market is complex, fragmented, and competitive; no single country or company is capable of exerting decisive influence over the market."[90] Russia's monopoly of natural gas in most ECE countries, as seen in Chapter 1, proves Rutland wrong.[91] Fiona Hill, director of the Center on the United States and Europe at Brookings, explained that in the 21st century Russia is poised to become an "energy superpower," but not in oil:

> Russia's energy future is in natural gas. As the next decade unfolds, continued crises in the Middle East and growing concern about pollution and global climate change will inevitably focus attention on Russia's vast reserves of cheaper, cleaner natural gas.[92]

Because the export of natural gas serves a political goal,[93] energy is of central significance for the Russian leadership, and maintaining the monopoly on the pipelines of natural gas to Eastern and Central Europe is at the core of Russia's national security policies. To this end, Edward Lucas identifies four goals that Russia has in order to maintain its monopoly on natural gas trade in Europe: first, "the Kremlin wants to prevent European countries from diversifying their sources of energy supply, particularly in gas"; second, "it wants to strengthen its hold over the international gas market"; third, "it wants to acquire downstream assets — distribution and storage capability — in Western countries"; and finally, "it wants to use those assets to exert political pressure."[94] Lucas is not alone in this conviction; Lin's research also indicates that Russia's NSS is based on maintaining Europe's dependence on Russian natural gas "via monopolistic control of pipelines and acquisition of transit countries' internal distribution networks."[95] These goals are further reinforced by Paul Domjan, who wrote that the main pillar of Russia's NSS until 2020, the Foreign Policy Concept, and Energy Strategy through 2030, is Russia's control of the natural gas transportation network and export pipelines to Europe:

> The government's control of export pipelines . . . is a matter of geopolitics and history: not only has geography blessed Russia with a prime location between an energy-producing region (Central Asia and West Siberia) and an energy-consuming region (Europe), but political complications, some deliberately initiated by the Russian government, have prevented the full realization of a southern energy corridor that would bypass Russia by way of the Caspian Sea, the Caucasus and Turkey. Moreover, the enormous network of . . . gas pipelines transiting Russian territory is a legacy of Russian political dominance. [96]

Domjan further stressed that the curse of the Eurasian landmass has been that the Russian natural gas export pipeline networks and the quasi-state-owned company that controls them—Gazprom—serve as "state-sanctioned chokepoints" against other nations for whom these same pipelines have historically been the only option to export or to have access to natural gas.[97] Fiona Hill also emphasized that "all existing pipeline routes run through Russia," but blamed this on the failure of Western companies to "make the same inroads into Caspian Asian gas production as they have in Caspian oil."[98] It is this failure that allows Russia today to "use gas as a political weapon to blackmail a neighboring consumer state that depends heavily on Russian supplies of natural gas."[99] Not surprisingly, the Energy Strategy of Russia through 2030, the Foreign Policy Concept, and the NSS of the Russian Federation until 2020 all placed the energy sector—and particularly natural gas—at the core of Russian diplomacy.[100]

The National Security Strategy of the Russian Federation until 2020 (NSS), approved by Medvedev in May 2009, asserts that Russia's national security depends above all on energy security—which relies on Europe's dependency on Russian natural gas, and on the economic benefits associated with profits from oil. Russia's principal goals by 2020 are to become "the world's fifth largest economy in terms of GDP"[101]— through the profits derived from export of overpriced oil—and to "develop into a global power"—by securing its monopoly of natural gas to ECE. Both of these goals depend on future energy supply and demand.[102] Because of this, energy security is closely identified with national security; the NSS warning that "competition for energy resources might create tension," which could even lead to military confrontations, particularly in the "Near Abroad," and in Russia's sphere of influence.[103] But while the NSS and the Russian political elite argue that Russia's great-power status is inherent in its military and economic potential,[104] in reality, this potential is almost nonexistent; leaving the energy sector as the main source of Russian power and influence.

The Russian military capabilities have been dramatically diminished after the collapse of the Soviet Union, and continued on this downward path during the Putin era—despite major investments in new military research and development. This fact is recognized not only by American academia and the intelligence community, but by much of Russia's own academia and political elite. Talking about Russian public opinion with regard to Russia's military strength, Vladimir Baranovsky wrote that this downward trend "is by and large considered irreversible."[105] According to Bernard Cole, at the grand strategic level Russia remains very much a major security concern for the United States and its allies, but not because of its military capabilities, but because of "the remaining Russian nuclear stockpile, and the problematic security of that stockpile." Edward Lucas even went a step further and wrote that "the nuclear arsenal and conventional forces are more a background psychological factor than a physical one."[106] At the tactical level, the Russian soldiers, along with their military commanders, generate revenues by selling fuel and equipment and by working for local enterprises in order to survive.[107] At all levels, the Russian military strength is characterized by helplessness:

> In its decrepit, drunken, demoralized military, bullying (hazing) is endemic. On average 12 Russian soldiers commit suicide every month. Russia's newest warplanes are formidably maneuverable, its submarines super silent, its torpedoes terrifyingly fast; but it has not yet been able to produce these brilliantly designed weapons in any quantities. Those in service are under deployed. Only the strategic nuclear arsenal gives Russia the right to call itself a military superpower. But two thirds of its missiles are obsolete. The Kremlin's ability to launch a disabling nuclear first strike on NATO has disappeared into the history books. So has its capacity to project military power around the globe, or even to launch a crippling conventional attack on Europe. In so far as a nuclear threat still exists, it is that paranoia and incompetence might lead to an accidental conflagration.[108]

The military decline was further exacerbated by the unprecedented deterioration in the standard of living, which will continue to worsen during the current financial crisis. While Russia is a member of the "G-8 club of big, rich, western countries,"[109] at home, Russian workers are increasingly convinced that "life was better when Russia was run by the Communists."[110] The bottom line is that Russia remains too weak and too poor to impose its will through "high explosives, hardened steel, and enriched uranium."[111] Because of this, energy security and geo-economics occupy the top priority of Russia's NSS: "National interests are identified mostly in terms of power—economic, military, informational, and political; not values, which are expedient and malleable. The power of gas . . . is more fungible than the power of nuclear weapons."[112]

The resurgence of Russia as a great power and its growing function as an energy superpower is also asserted in the most recent *Foreign Policy Concept*, which was signed into law by Medvedev in July 2008. Christian Thorun, founder and managing director of ConPolicy, believes that the Russian leadership's current foreign policy thinking is in fact a continuation of Putin's legacy. During his presidency, Putin understood that "only an economically strong Russia would be taken seriously in the international arena and that economic power would significantly expand the tools available to Russian foreign-policy."[113] But Putin's pragmatic geo-economic realism "seems impossible"[114] to materialize without access to Russia's vast energy resources, in particular to its natural gas. Russian security expert Marcel de Haas—author of the first edition of the *Netherlands Defense Doctrine*—emphasized this element of the Foreign Policy Concept:

> The Foreign Policy Concept devoted considerable attention to energy, both in terms of security issues and resources. This approach was also in line with Putin's 2007 and 2008 statements. Energy became a consistent part of Moscow's security thinking due to its ability to produce high revenues and its use as an instrument

of power, particularly during the gas conflicts with Ukraine.[115]

Finally, *the Energy Strategy of Russia through 2030* also identifies energy security as "one of the most important components of the national security"[116] and defines it as the "protection of the country, its citizens, society, state and economy" against the threats to both energy supply and demand.[117] Because of this, energy security "must be provided without prejudice to any national interests whatsoever."[118] The main external risks (geopolitical, macroeconomic, and market)[119] to energy security are identified as "volatility of world prices, increasing competition at traditional markets, low diversification of export, and transit dependency,"[120] and will determine "Russia's future position on the world energy markets."[121] Furthermore, the document predicts that for the next 2 decades, Russia will "undeniably remain the leading player on the world hydrocarbon market"[122] — particularly due to Europe's increasing demand for natural gas[123] — and that the energy sector "will retain its crucial role in resolving the important strategic task"[124] of geo-economic stability:

> Russia will thus not only retain its position as the largest energy supplier in the world, but will also qualitatively change its presence on the world energy market by diversifying its commodities structure and destinations of energy export, actively developing new international energy business and increasing the presence of Russian companies abroad. . . . The strategic objective of the foreign energy policy is the maximum efficient use of the Russian energy potential.[125]

WHY AND HOW DOES RUSSIA USE NATURAL GAS AS AN INSTRUMENT OF COERCION IN ITS SPHERE OF INFLUENCE?

Since the end of World War II, with the Long Telegram of George Kennan—the father of containment, who wrote that "no single Continental land power should come to dominate the entire Eurasian landmass"—until the end of the Cold War, with President Bush asserting that containment was meant "to prevent any hostile power or group of powers from dominating the Eurasian landmass,"[126] politicians, historians, and academics have viewed ECE as the "strategic heartland of the great European landmass."[127] All these voices resonate with Halford Mackinder's theory that: "Who rules East Europe commands the Heartland; Who rules the Heartland commands the World Island; Who rules the World Island commands the World."[128] Indeed, all these assertions have proven to be historically accurate, and for this reason, ECE continues to be considered of great geostrategic significance for the security and stability of the Eurasian supercontinent:

> In the 19th Century, they were objects of intense interest to the large empires on their periphery: Germany, Russia, Austria, and Turkey. Because events in Central/Eastern Europe were at the root of the two world wars, political development in the region is important to the security of not only Germany, the Scandinavian countries, and Russia and the Eurasian republics, but also to the states of Western Europe.[129]

Ronald Reagan, who once described the Soviet Union as an "evil empire," understood very well that a Kremlin-controlled European natural gas pipeline infrastructure would provide the USSR with a great opportunity to control not only Eastern Europe, but the entire European continent. For this reason, during his first term in office, Reagan attempted—although unsuccessfully—to stop the first natural gas pipeline from being built between Russia and Germany.[130] His legacy seems long forgotten today, when many energy security experts assert that "we live in a more benign world,"[131] where conquest of land is highly unprofitable—persuading rulers to consider physical geography as politically neutral. Colin Gray also agreed with this assertion, but he pointed out that those who adapt best "to the terms and conditions of life and warfare in the jungle, will count that particular terrain as an ally rather than as a 'neutral' geographical stage."[132] In the dominion of Russian resource nationalism, state capitalists like Putin look at geography as an ally whose natural gas resources become a means of advancing Russia's grand strategic ends in its sphere of influence.[133]

While most ECE nations historically have depended on Soviet natural gas,[134] in the contemporary security environment Russian natural gas exports *dominate* "both on the European gas market and on the gas market of the Commonwealth of Independent States."[135] Virginia Comolli, from the International Institute for Strategic Studies (IISS), believes that this dominance "heightens the tendency to use energy superiority for political purposes and to underline Russia's claim to be a major force in international relations."[136] The significance of natural gas for Russia's foreign policy is, on the one hand, the result of a structurally weak economy dependent on the export of hydrocarbons,[137] and on the other, the result of Russia's strategic goal to secure its traditional sphere of influence. As seen in Russia's national strategies, geo-economic considerations act as a pillar of Russia's foreign policy, and economic growth itself depends on Russia's sphere of influence. This is especially evident in the natural gas sector. Russia's role as the main natural gas exporter to Europe—and for some European states, the only exporter of natural gas—and the significance of natural gas to Russia's own economic development "has inevitably influenced Russia's foreign-policy."[138] According to Jane's Country Risk Assessment—and as illustrated in the first chapter of this monograph—this monopoly power indeed "extends beyond Russia's borders, with countries such as Belarus, Finland, Turkey, Slovakia, the Czech Republic, Ukraine, Poland, and Austria relying on [Russia] for over half of their gas imports."[139] These facts persuaded scholars like Kazantsev to assert that "gas is a backbone not only of Russian foreign policy, but also of the domestic political system."[140] Consequently, Russia needs to maintain its sphere of influence for economic and geopolitical considerations (both domestic and international), and it needs to maintain its monopoly of natural gas in ECE states in order to retain control over this sphere of influence. Any attempt by ECE countries to circumvent this dependence on Russian natural gas will thus be met with much resistance by the Russian political elite:

> Russia was, and still is, alarmed by the possibility of cheap Central Asian gas appearing on European markets because it would compete with Gazprom's gas. A related fear was the danger of the South Caucasus being used for the transportation of Central Asian gas (through a Transcaspian gas pipeline and the Nabucco project) to Europe. As a result of this, Russian geopolitical power in the CIS serves the commercial purpose of keeping Gazprom's position in European gas mar-

kets. So power considerations were mixed with the aspiration for profits, as it was in the case of European trade companies of the Early Modern period.[141]

What is even more alarming is that 60 percent of the Russian public supports reestablishing Soviet-era control over ECE countries; a threat that Keith Smith — former U.S. Ambassador to Lithuania and currently a senior associate in the CSIS New European Democracies Project — believes "cannot be dismissed."[142] President Medvedev himself expects the West to accept that Russia has "privileged interests in certain regions," particularly in the post-Soviet space and, *in extremis*, ECE.[143] To this end, natural gas has become the preferred tool of Russian diplomacy, "making it subject to [the] Kremlin's political strategy rather than commercial needs";[144] Prime Minister Putin being by far the most assertive promoter of using natural gas "to coerce the consuming countries."[145]

Russia stands accused today of using natural gas as an instrument of state power. Indeed, over the past decade, several ECE countries have experienced "the suspension or reduction of . . . gas flows from Russia coincident with political or economic disputes."[146] And as it will be shown, in Ukraine's case, in which natural gas was used as an instrument of coercion — particularly in the context of economic incentives and penalties,[147] or by "withholding or threatening to withhold" vital natural gas shipments[148] — this type of unilateral sanction was very effective.

ENDNOTES - CHAPTER 2

1. Edward Lucas, *The New Cold War: Putin's Russia and the Threat to the West*, New York: Palgrave MacMillan, 2009, p. 164.

2. David Knott, "Black Cloud Over White Night," *Oil & Gas Journal,* November 8, 1993, p. 32.

3. Russia's perception of NATO as hostile is clear despite recent claims by the NATO-Russia Council Joint Statement, which spoke of a "new stage of cooperation towards a true strategic partnership" and that "the security of NATO and Russia is intertwined." These statements completely ignored the words of President Medvedev at the Lisbon NRC Summit, who pointed out that "Russia would participate only on an absolutely equal basis"; only as long as it benefits Russia's foreign policy interests. Pavel Petrovsky and Vladimir Dedushkin, "Quo Vadis, NATO? A Glance from Lisbon," *International Affairs*, Vol. 57, No. 1, 2011, pp. 49-57.

4. The two natural gas pipelines that will further increase Russia's ability to use natural gas as an instrument of coercion, Nord Stream and South Stream, are expected to cost between €23-28 billion, and profitability was not a major factor in the decision to build them. In fact, Zeyno Baran argued that the Nord Stream pipeline alone will cost several times more than a proposed overland project would have. Zeyno Baran, "EU Energy Security: Time to End Russian Leverage," *Washington Quarterly*, Vol. 30, No. 4, October, 2007, p. 135; Christina Lin, *The Prince of Rosh: Russian Energy Imperialism and the Emerging Eurasian Military Alliance of the Shanghai Cooperation Organization,* Berlin, Germany: Institute for Strategic-Political-Security-and Economic Consultancy (ISP-SW), 2009.

5. Stephen F. Larrabee, "Russia, Ukraine, and Central Europe: The Return of Geopolitics." *Journal of International Affairs*, Vol. 63, No. 2, Spring 2010, p. 33.

6. For the purpose of this chapter, ECE is comprised of the Baltic Republics (Estonia, Latvia, and Lithuania); Central Europe (Poland, the Czech Republic, Slovakia, and Hungary); the Balkans (Serbia and Montenegro, Slovenia, Croatia, Bosnia-Herzegovina, Macedonia, and Albania); and Southeastern Europe (Romania and Bulgaria). Wayne Thompson, *Nordic, Central, and Southeastern Europe*, 5th Ed., Harpers Ferry, WV: Stryker-Post Publications, 2005.

7. Frederic Labarre, "Russian Neo-Mercantilism," 10th CDAI Graduate Symposium, Kingston, Ontario, Canada, October 27, 2007, p. 2.

8. The Russian Institute of Contemporary Development (IN-SOR) is a Moscow-based think tank affiliated with Russian President Dmitry Medvedev.

9. Andrey Kazantsev, "The Crisis of GAZPROM as the Crisis of Russia's Energy Superstate Policy Towards Europe and the Former Soviet Union," *Caucasian Review of International Affairs*, Vol. 4, No. 3, Summer 2010, p. 281.

10. Vladimir Baranovsky, "Russia: A Part of Europe Or Apart from Europe?" *International Affairs*, Vol. 76, No. 3, July 2000, p. 443.

11. Matthew Clements, ed., *Country Risk Assessments. Russia and the CIS*, 24th Ed., Alexandria, VA: Jane's Sentinel, 2009, p. 479.

12. Jerrold Schecter, *Russian Negotiating Behavior*, Washington, DC: United States Institute of Peace Press, 1998, p. 49.

13. Christian Thorun, *Explaining Change in Russian Foreign Policy. The Role of Ideas in Post-Soviet Russia's Conduct Towards the West*, New York: Palgrave MacMillan, 2009, p. 37.

14. Schecter, p. 45.

15. Thorun, p. 151.

16. Ian Bremmer, *The End of the Free Market*, New York: Penguin Group, 2010, p. 53.

17. Stephen K. Wegren and Dale R. Herspring, eds, *After Putin's Russia. Past Imperfect, Future Uncertain*, 4th Ed., Plymouth, UK: Rowman & Littlefield Publishers, Inc., 2010, p. 318.

18. Andrei P. Tsygankov and Pavel A. Tsygankov, "National Ideology and IR Theory: Three Incarnations of the 'Russian Idea'," *European Journal of International Relations*, Vol. 16, No. 4, December 2010, p. 670.

19. Viatcheslav Morozov, "Imperial Discourse in Russian International Studies: Empire Vs. the Corporatist State as Images of Putin's Russia," 4th CEEISA Convention, Tartu, Estonia, June 26, 2006, p. 6.

20. Lin.

21. Alexandre Mansourov, "Mercantilism and Neo-Imperialism in Russian Foreign Policy during President Putin's 2nd Term," *The Korean Journal of Defense Analysis*, Vol. 17, No. 1, Spring, 2005, p. 158.

22. Tsygankov and Tsygankov, p. 676.

23. Mansourov, p. 158.

24. Tsygankov and Tsygankov, p. 676.

25. Andrei Tsygankov, "Russia's Foreign Policy," in Stephen K. Wegren and Dale R. Herspring, eds., p. 223.

26. *Country Risk Assessments, Russia and the CIS,* p. 479.

27. Thorun, p. 151.

28. *Country Risk Assessments,. Russia and the CIS,* p. 482.

29. Baranovsky, p. 452.

30. Lucas.

31. Minton Goldman, ed., *Russia, The Eurasian Republics, and Central/Eastern Europe*, 10th Ed., Dubuque, IA: Global Studies, 2005, p. 100.

32. Lucas, p. 131.

33. Goldman, p. 55.

34. *Ibid*.

35. Lucas, p. 131.

36. *Country Risk Assessments, Russia and the CIS,* p. 482.

37. Goldman, p. 75.

38. *Ibid.*

39. "Opinion Poll: Nationalism in Contemporary Russia," *Russian Analytical Digest,* Vol. 93, March 10, 2011, pp. 10-11.

40. Lucas, p. 131.

41. *Country Risk Assessments,* p. 479.

42. H. J. Mackinder, "The Geographical Pivot of History," *The Geographical Journal,* Vol. 23, No. 4, April 1904, pp. 421-437.

43. *Ibid.*

44. Lin, p. 1.

45. Two things stand out from the very first page of the dissertation: first, that Putin's field of study was Economics and the Management of the National Economy; and second, the name of the study itself was titled "The Strategic Planning of Regional Natural Resources under the Formation of Market Relations."

46. Vladimir Vladimirovich Putin, "The Strategic Planning of Regional Natural Resources Under the Formation of Market Relations," Ph.D. Thesis in Economics, Saint Petersburg State Mining University, pp. 1-218.

47. The International Energy Forum, the world's largest gathering of Energy Ministers, defines resource nationalism as ". . . nations wanting to make the most of their endowment." Paul Stevens, "National Oil Companies and International Oil Companies in the Middle East: Under the Shadow of Government and the Resource Nationalism Cycle," *Journal of World Energy Law & Business,* Vol. 12, No. 1, 2008, p. 5. Resource nationalism requires said nations to "shift political and economic control of their energy and mining sectors from foreign and private interests to domestic and state controlled companies." Ian Bremmer and Robert Johnston, "The Rise and Fall of Resource Nationalism," *Survival,* Vol. 51,

No. 2, April, 2009, pp. 149-158. This has also been emphasized by Professor Paul Stevens, Senior Research Fellow on Energy at the Chatham House, the home of the Royal Institute for International Affairs, who wrote that resource nationalism has been historically characterized by "a battle between national interests and foreign influences." Stevens, p. 8. This has been the case in Russia.

48. Bremmer, *The End of the Free Market*, p. 107.

49. *Ibid.*, p. 33.

50. *Ibid.*, p. 34.

51. *Ibid.*, p. 41.

52. *Ibid.*, p. 37.

53. *Ibid.*, p. 52.

54. Ernest Raiklin, *After Gorbachev? A Mechanism for the Transformation of Totalitarian State Capitalism into Authoritarian Mixed Capitalism*, Washington, DC: Council for Social and Economic Studies, 1989, p. 105.

55. Bremmer, *The End of the Free Market*, p. 39.

56. *Ibid.*, p. 53.

57. *Ibid.*, p. 107.

58. *Ibid.*, p. 6.

59. *Ibid.*, p. 5.

60. *Ibid.*, p. 5.

61. *Ibid.*, p. 63.

62. Ian Bremmer, "The Return of State Capitalism," *Survival*, Vol. 50, No. 3, June 2008, pp. 55-64.

63. *Ibid.*

64. In many cases, foreign investors must gain approval from a government commission advised by the Federal Security Bureau, the former KGB, headed by Prime Minister Putin, before buying assets considered of national and/or strategic significance. *Ibid.*

65. Kazantsev, p. 271.

66. *Ibid.*, p. 271.

67. Paul Domjan and Matt Stone, "A Comparative Study of Resource Nationalism in Russia and Kazakhstan 2004-2008," *Europe-Asia Studies*, Vol. 62, No. 1, January 6, 2010, p. 43.

68. Kazantsev, p. 284.

69. Bremmer, *The End of the Free Market*, p. 107.

70. Domjan and Stone, p. 35.

71. Bremmer, *The End of the Free Market*, p. 63.

72. Domjan and Stone, p. 36.

73. Bremmer, *The End of the Free Market*, p. 63.

74. Domjan and Stone, p. 36.

75. Bremmer, *The End of the Free Market*, p. 63.

76. Kazantsev, p. 271.

77. Domjan and Stone, p. 38.

78. *Ibid.*, p. 40.

79. *Ibid.*, p. 38.

80. *Ibid.*, p. 39.

81. *Ibid.*

82. Bremmer, *The End of the Free Market*, p. 52.

83. Domjan and Stone, p. 36.

84. Lucas, p. 163.

85. Thorun, p. 31.

86. Virginia Comolli, "Energy Security," in *Europe and Global Security*, Bastian Giegerich, ed., London, UK: International Institute for Strategic Studies, 2010, p. 188.

87. *The Energy Strategy of Russia through 2030*, p. 21.

88. Kazantsev, p. 274.

89. Fiona Hill, "Russia: The 21st Century's Energy Superpower?" in *Russia. the Eurasian Republics, and Central/Eastern Europe,* 10th Ed., Milton Goldman, ed., Dubuque, IA: Global Studies, 2005, p. 220.

90. Peter Rutland, "Russia as an Energy Superpower," *New Political Economy*, Vol. 13, No. 2, June 2008, p. 207.

91. But even if we combine oil and gas together, by Russia's own admission, it controls 23 percent of the world's oil and natural gas reserves, making it the world's richest nation in terms of hydrocarbon reserves. In oil alone, by Rutland's own admission, Russia ties with Saudi Arabia for first place in production.

92. Hill, p. 220.

93. Sophia Dimitrakopoulou and Andrew Liaropoulos, "Russia's National Security Strategy to 2020: A Great Power in the Making?" *Caucasian Review of International Affairs*, Vol. 4, No. 1, Winter, 2010, p. 38.

94. Lucas, p. 163.

95. Lin, p. 2.

96. Domjan and Stone, p. 40.

97. *Ibid.*, p. 41.

98. Hill, p. 222.

99. Kazantsev, p. 274.

100. Sophia Dimitrakopoulou argued that "the National Security Strategy reflects the restoration of Russia's Great Power identity (*derzhavnost*) that took place during the Putin era," Dimitrakopoulou and Liaropoulos, p. 42.

101. *Ibid.*, p. 38.

102. Marcel de Haas, "Medvedev's Security Policy: A Provisional Assessment," *Russian Analytical Digest*, Vol. 62, June 18, 2009, p. 3.

103. *Ibid.*, p. 3. Also emphasizing the views of David Victor, former director of the Program on Energy and Sustainable Development at the Freeman Spogli Institute for International Studies at Stanford University, who wrote that "the world may be headed for a spate of resource wars, hot conflicts triggered by a struggle to grab valuable resources." David G. Victor, "What Resource Wars?" *National Interest*, No. 92, November, 2007, p. 48.

104. Thorun, p. 37.

105. Baranovsky, p. 449.

106. Lucas, p. 10.

107. Goldman, p. 47.

108. Lucas, p. 5.

109. *Ibid.*, p. 4.

110. Goldman, 45.

111. Lucas, p. 10.

112. Mansourov, p. 152.

113. Thorun, p. 31.

114. Baranovsky, p. 449.

115. de Haas, p. 2.

116. *The Energy Strategy of Russia through 2030*, Moscow, Russia: Ministry of Energy of the Russian Federation, 2010.

117. *Ibid.*; Nikolay Kaveshnikov, "The Issue of Energy Security in Relations between Russia and the European Union," *European Security*, Vol. 19, No. 4, December 2010, p. 587.

118. *The Energy Strategy of Russia through 2030*, p. 22.

119. *Ibid.*

120. *Ibid.*; Kaveshnikov, p. 587.

121. *The Energy Strategy of Russia through 2030*, p. 22.

122. *Ibid.*

123. A fact also emphasized by Alexander Medvedev, deputy chairman of OAO Gazprom Management Committee and Director General of OOO Gazprom Export, who just this year reminded the world that "most forecasts by leading consulting agencies, government organizations, and industry associations point to an increase in European gas demand over the long term. According to the consensus forecast, demand for gas in the European countries will reach 637 bcm in 2020 and 648 bcm by 2030." Alexander Medvedev, "The Economic Crisis and the Future of the Gas Sector," *International Affairs*, Vol. 57, No. 1, 2011, pp. 188-191.

124. Kaveshnikov, p. 594.

125. *The Energy Strategy of Russia through 2030*, p. 55.

126. Peter Liberman, "The Spoils of Conquest," *International Security*, Vol. 18, No. 2, Fall 1993, p. 129.

127. Goldman, p. 88.

128. Liberman, p. 127.

129. Goldman, p. 88.

130. Lin, p. 2.

131. Liberman, p. 125.

132. Colin Gray, "Inescapable Geography," *Journal of Strategic Studies*, Vol. 22, No. 2, 1999, p. 173.

133. Edward Lucas identified this sphere of influence as "the countries bordering Russia, starting with those covered by the 1939 Molotov-Ribbentrop Pact — the Baltic States, Central Europe, and the Balkans — but reaching around the Black Sea to the Caucasus." This, he argued, is the main theater of the New Cold War. Lucas, p. 129.

134. Goldman, p. 101.

135. *The Energy Strategy of Russia through 2030*, p. 21.

136. Comolli, p. 188.

137. Kazantsev, p. 274.

138. Hill, p. 221.

139. *Country Risk Assessments, Russia and the CIS*, p. 472.

140. Kazantsev, p. 280. Andrey Kazantsev also argued that "there was also a very important peculiar feature of the gas sector in Russia: only in this sector of the economy where there was such a strong link between Russia's domestic economic and foreign policies."

141. *Ibid.*, p. 275.

142. Keith Smith, *Russia-Europe Energy Relations. Implications for U.S. Policy*, Washington, DC: CSIS, 2010.

143. Larrabee, p. 37.

144. *Country Risk Assessments, Russia and the CIS*, p. 472.

145. Smith, p. 9.

146. Domjan and Stone, p. 44.

147. Lucas, p. 159.

148. Smith, p. 1.

CHAPTER 3

CARROTS AND STICKS:
A LOOK AT RUSSIA-UKRAINE GAS PIPELINE
POLITICS

Without Ukraine, Russia is a desperately defensive
power, lacking any natural defenses aside from sheer
distance.[1]

Peter Zeihan

In the midst of the cold European winter of 2009,
on January 7, Russia cut off its supplies of natural gas
to Ukraine for 14 days, causing natural gas shortfalls
in over 20 countries.[2] Russia stands accused of using
natural gas to advance its foreign policy objectives by
taking advantage of Ukraine's susceptibility to Russian coercion (see Figure 4-1). Hrygoriy Perepelytsya —
Military Department Director of the Kyiv National
Institute for Strategic Studies (NISS) — explained that
this cutoff came as a result of Russia's strategic move
to damage the reputation of the Ukrainian Orange
Revolution, which Russian President Dmitry Medvedev perceived as contrary to Russian interests:

> From 2005 till 2009, the main tasks of Russia in foreign
> policy were to discredit [the] current government and,
> first of all its President Viktor Yuschenko as personifi-
> cation of orange power, and to disgrace [the] Orange
> revolution's ideals in the eyes of [its] own citizens of
> Ukraine and [the] international community. Russian
> and Ukrainian society were obtruded the opinion on
> the falseness of democratic choice and European in-
> tegration aspirations, and Yuschenko by himself . . .
> performed as [an] American marionette.[3]

Russia's strategy was very effective: A 2008 opinion poll by the Ukrainian Centre of Economic and Political Studies indicated that between 2003 and 2008, the Ukrainian perception toward Russia was radically transformed; with 51 percent of Ukrainians believing that good relations with Russia should be the top priority of Ukrainian foreign policy in December 2008, as opposed to only 28 percent in September 2003.[4] Furthermore, according to a 2010 poll by the Levada Centre, "the absolute majority (92 percent) claimed their respect for Russia . . . bad feelings towards Russia was claimed by only 6 percent of interviewed Ukrainians."[5] Russia successfully suppressed the Orange Revolution without firing a shot, but by patiently using natural gas as its instrument of state power.[6]

Russia no longer possesses the capacity to enforce its grand strategic ends through the use of military force. Peter Zeihan, Vice President of Analysis for Strategic Forcasting, Inc. (STRATFOR), accurately portrayed in the quote that opened this chapter the way many American geopolitical and intelligence professionals analyze Russia-Ukraine relations: underestimating Russian power and overestimating its vulnerabilities. The tendency to understate the influence Russia still has in Russia's *near abroad* is also apparent in Zbigniew Brzezinski's analysis that "without Ukraine, Russia ceases to be an empire, but with Ukraine suborned and then subordinated, Russia automatically becomes an empire."[7] While Russia needs to maintain control over its sphere of influence for both political and economic reasons—as discussed in Chapter 2—this chapter will show that American geopolitical analysts who agree with Zeihan and Brzezinski fail to understand the shift in the preferred Russian methods of solving disputes in the contemporary security environment.

Both Zeihan and Brzezinski look at Russia from a traditional security mindset, focusing on the weakness of the Russian military power. With regard to the Russia-Ukraine relationship, both authors fail to acknowledge the importance of Ukraine's gas infrastructure for Russia[8] (80 percent[9] of the Caucasus gas exported by Russia to Western Europe passed through Ukraine), Ukraine's role as a gas supply regulator (Ukraine's extensive gas storage capabilities are vital in guaranteeing that Russian contracted gas reaches Western Europe despite seasonal fluctuations),[10] and the fact that Ukraine imports 14.98 percent of Russian total gas exports—as seen in Figure 3-3. To use Albert Hirschman's logic,[11] a look at Ukraine as the main transit country for Russian gas to Europe presents a strong argument for Russia to use unilateral economic sanctions as a means to solidify Russian control of the Ukrainian gas infrastructure. Ukraine's own vulnerability to the disruption of gas supplies remains crucial in solidifying this control.

To fully understand the "pattern"[12] of Russia using natural gas as an instrument of economic coercion, it is helpful to recognize three of Moscow's demands of Ukraine after the fall of the Soviet Union:[13] (1) renunciation of its claims to the Soviet nuclear stockpile in Ukraine, and the surrender of all nuclear warheads to Russia; (2) recognition of Russia as the legal inheritor of all political, economic and military infrastructure belonging to the Soviet Union, to include exclusive rights to the Ukrainian pipeline infrastructure and to the Black Sea fleet and the port of Sevastopol; and (3) recognition of Russia as the regional hegemon.[14]

MOSCOW'S FIRST DEMAND: RENUNCIATION OF ITS CLAIMS TO THE SOVIET NUCLEAR STOCKPILE[15]

It is largely agreed in academic literature that Russia's use of natural gas as an instrument of economic coercion has failed in the enforcement of the first demand.[16] This episode is, however, important to discuss in order to establish a pattern in the use of this particular type of coercion. A series of events described in depth in Drezner's writings come to mind:

- In 1992, popular support for retaining the Ukrainian nuclear deterrent is on the rise,[17] and Ukraine declares legal ownership of the nuclear stockpile.[18]
- In February 1993, the Russian government threatens for the first time to raise the price of gas. Shortly after, the gas prices rise tenfold from $4 to $40 per 1,000 cubic meters.[19]
- In September 1993, gas supplies to Ukraine decrease by 25 percent. Russian President Yeltsin threatens to completely cut off gas shipments if Ukraine fails to make concessions on Russia's demand for the Ukraine to relinquish its nuclear stockpiles.[20]

Despite these facts, Drezner argued that Russia's first demand was not settled by the means of coercion, but by diplomatic means. In January 1994, the United States brokered a final agreement between Russia and Ukraine,[21] whereas the latter would surrender its nuclear stockpile, and with it, its nuclear ambitions.[22] This caused some scholars, including Drezner, to conclude that the use of gas as a national security coercive instrument, especially when coupled with military pressure—at that time Ukraine still feared a Russian military offensive,[23] because Senior Russian officials kept describing Ukraine's independence as a temporary phenomenon[24]—would "produce the fewest concessions" from Ukraine.[25] Drezner's evaluations are, however, arguably subjective, and largely based on a one-sided traditional approach that fails to recognize the bigger strategic design of economic sanctions.[26]

First, Drezner's argument does not consider the fact that by 1994, almost half of Ukraine's population supported retaining the Ukrainian nuclear deterrent.[27] At the individual level of analysis, it is hard to believe that Ukraine's leaders simply chose to ignore half of the electorate just because the United States provided written guarantees that it would protect Ukraine against Russia in the event of a regional conflict. This was an unpopular move that could have resulted in a loss of popular support.[28]

Second, Drezner, admits that, "by February 1994, Ukraine owed Russia $3.4 billion; an immediate halt to all energy subsidies would have cut Ukraine's GNP [Gross National Product] by 3.5%."[29] It seems again impossible that the Ukrainian policymakers did not consider the economic implications of refusing Russia's demands.

Third, Drezner fails to acknowledge the twofold purpose of the unilateral economic sanctions:[30] the target of the Russian Government was not only Ukraine, but also the Russian Parliament.[31] In 1990, 73 of 79 billion cubic meters (bcm) of gas per year were delivered to Western Europe via Ukraine.[32] With the export of gas being the main sources of revenue for Russia, the risk of over 90 percent of it depending on Ukrainian collaboration forced Russian policymakers to consider alternative transit routes to Europe.[33] This is partly why projects like Yamal-Europe through Belarus and Poland, Nord Stream through the Baltic Sea, and South Stream through the Black Sea were considered; "to strengthen Russian influence in Europe."[34]

Ultimately, Drezner failed to acknowledge the impact of gas disruptions on Ukraine's decision to transfer its nuclear weapons to Russia.[35] The fact that negotiations were concluded with the help of the United States does not mean that threats of gas disruption were ineffective. There is no proof to show that Ukrainian politicians used U.S. mediation as political cover so that it did not look like total capitulation, and this chapter does not intend to demonstrate that this was the case. Instead, it intends to show that natural gas as an instrument of coercion was used successfully, even though it was not the only tool used during the negotiations.

The effectiveness of gas as an instrument of coercion becomes more apparent in negotiations involving the last two demands made by Russia to Ukraine. A carrots-and-sticks strategy can also be identified in the way Russia approached these issues. For example, Russia's second demand was resolved using natural gas as an incentive to move along negotiations with a friendly Ukraine, while the second demand favored the use of deadlocks in dealing with a belligerent Ukraine.

MOSCOW'S SECOND DEMAND: RECOGNITION OF RUSSIA AS THE LEGAL INHERITOR OF SOVIET MILITARY AND GOVERNMENT PROPERTY, EQUIPMENT, AND NATURAL GAS INFRASTRUCTURE IN UKRAINE

A close look at Ukraine since the election of the pro-Russian Viktor Yanukovych in February 2010 reveals that, in dealing with a friendly Ukraine, gas-related incentives rather than pure threats were favored in pursuing Russia's national security objectives at the Black Sea.[36] This use of incentives, often even coupled with threats, has been successfully employed by Russia to obtain exclusive rights to the Ukrainian pipeline infrastructure[37] and to the port of Sevastopol.

Negotiations for the purchase of the Sevastopol fleet and for exclusive rights to the port of Sevastopol have been well-documented; they substantiate this use of gas as both an incentive and as an instrument of coercion even before the pro-Russian Yanukovych took power:

1. Demand of the Sevastopol Fleet: The 1993 demand for the Sevastopol fleet and basing rights came with an offer to forgive Ukraine's gas debts to Russia. It also came with the use of gas dependence as an intimidation tool, when Yeltsin threatened that the failure of Ukraine to cooperate will result in the disruption of the Russian gas supply.[38] The fleet demand was resolved during the Sochi Summit in 1994, when Ukraine sold most of its fleet to Russia. In return, Russia upheld its side of the bargain, and forgave most of Ukraine's gas debts.[39]

2. Demand of Basing Rights in Sevastopol: When the 1996 Ukrainian constitution barred the permanent stationing of Russian troops on Ukrainian territory,[40] Russia again threatened to raise the price of gas (as stated by the Ukrainian Foreign Minister).[41] Not surprisingly, in May 2007, a 20-year "lease" of the base was signed between the two sides[42] in exchange for a 10-year deferment on Ukraine's gas debts.[43]

Interestingly enough, after the pro-Russian Yanukovych took power, no outspoken threats were made in the conduct of negotiations over the port of Sevastopol. Natural gas was used as an incentive; while the instrument of coercion remained hidden in the background. The renewal of the Sevastopol port agreement in 2010 resulted in a 30-percent discount on gas prices,[44] and on September 30, 2010, it brought a modest adjustment on the amount of gas Ukraine is obligated to purchase.[45] The fact that the gas price discount was used as an incentive is not a secret:[46] After the conclusion of negotiations, the Russian President openly admitted that the 30-year lease of the Sevastopol base was "intimately interconnected" to the 10-year gas discount agreement.[47]

The fact that the flow of Russian natural gas was not interrupted to a friendly Ukraine does not mean, however, that Russia gave up its capabilities to employ gas as an instrument of coercion in the future. In fact, Russia was able to maintain its ability to threaten Ukraine in the future. Ukrainian authorities agree that a 30-percent discount on gas prices is really insignificant.[48] Even after the discount was applied, the Ukrainian Prime Minister Mykola Azarov still considered the Ukraine-Russia bilateral agreement on natural gas prices as "extremely unfavorable for Ukraine."[49]

Moreover, Naftogaz Ukrainy is still contracted to purchase double (41 bcm) the amount of gas than it can consume (22 bcm)[50] per year, while waiving the right to export its surplus without Gazprom's approval.[51] These bargaining chips were kept for use in upcoming negotiations on exclusive rights to the Ukrainian pipeline infrastructure (which was also part of Russia's demand of Ukraine after the fall of the Union of Soviet Socialist Republic [USSR]).[52]

Vladimir Putin stated that "Russian power in Eastern Europe depends on its role as Europe's energy arbiter," and Russian control of Ukraine's natural gas infrastructure is vital to Russia's grand strategic ends in its sphere of influence.[53] Richard Andres, Senior Fellow and Energy and Environment Security and Policy Chair at the Institute for National Strategic Studies (INSS), explained that Ukraine's natural gas transit infrastructure "would significantly boost Russia's ability to use gas as a political lever against states within the region,"[54] and the natural gas shortfalls in over 20 countries as a result of the 2009 cut off to Ukraine proves just that. Even Western nations were affected, with Southern Germany being starved of 60 percent of its imported natural gas (see Figure 3-1).

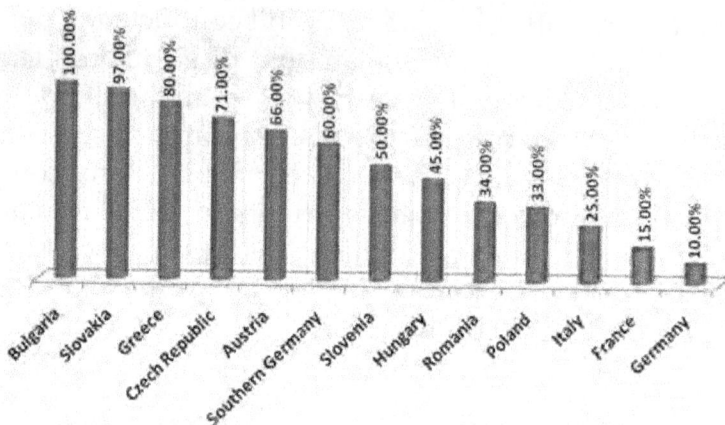

Source: the European Commission.[55]

Figure 3-1. Natural Gas Shortfalls by Country during the January 2009 Cutoff to Ukraine.

Recent developments indicate that the control of gas pipelines in ECE may become the focus of Russia over the next decade. This detail was emphasized by Russian Prime Minister Putin himself in April 2010, when he made public Russia's intent of a merger between Russia's Gazprom and Ukraine's Naftogaz.[56] Both companies are state-controlled; with Gazprom acting as the regional monopoly of gas.[57] During his 2006 State of the Nation speech, President Vladimir Putin called the growth of Gazprom "the result of a carefully planned action by the state."[58] Regaining control of the trans-Ukraine gas pipeline is of strategic importance to Russia because this route still transports 80 percent of its total gas exports to Western Europe (as of 2010).[59] In September 2010, the Ukrainian-Russian international consortium already lifted a ban that prohibited foreign companies from running the Ukrainian gas pipelines and initiated a bill that could allow Russian companies to control them.[60]

On October 27, Ukrainian Prime Minister Mykola Azarov, who holds a doctorate from the Moscow State University,[61] tried to push back. He described the intended merger between Gazprom and Naftogaz as a "takeover rather than a merger," while sources within the Ukrainian government described it an "absolute control of our [gas] transportation system."[62] This seems to be confirmed by a report of *The Economist* Intelligence unit, which warned that under the merger, Russia would also achieve full control of Ukraine's domestic gas production.[63] On November 1, however, Azarov declared that "both parties want to find the optimal conditions for this merger,"[64] and on April 12, 2011, Azarov told Russian Prime Minister Vladimir Putin that Ukraine is "interested in valuing related assets in the nearest future to find the best format and most appropriate terms of such a joint venture."[65]

Ultimately, the Russian demand to have exclusive rights to the port of Sevastopol, and to a certain extent to the Ukrainian pipeline infrastructure,[66] was resolved using gas-related incentives to move negotiations along. However, because of the mistrust between the two countries, the threat of gas disruption will remain constant in bilateral relations even with a friendly Ukraine: It insures that this friendly relation continues. A look at the Sevastopol affair clearly indicates this.

MOSCOW'S THIRD DEMAND: RECOGNITION OF RUSSIA AS REGIONAL HEGEMON

Ukraine's cooperation, and the use of incentives to acquire it, was not always the case in Russo-Ukrainian negotiations. The use of gas as a coercive instrument during the Orange Revolution in Ukraine clearly indicates this. The Orange Revolution was a direct affront to Russia's third demand of Ukraine; recognition of Russia as the protector of Russians living in Ukraine (comprising of 22 percent of Ukraine's population),[67] and recognition of its status as the regional hegemon. Not surprisingly, when pro-Western Viktor Yushchenko was elected president in 2004, Russian President Putin was quoted saying that "Ukraine should think twice about any such embrace of the West," and was quick to threaten that if Ukraine positioned itself against Russia, it might cost it a threefold increase in the price of gas (an average of $4 billion per year).[68] Putin even threatened Ukraine "with dismemberment if it persisted in trying to join the NATO alliance."[69]

With Ukraine relying on Russia for 51.6 percent of its domestic natural gas consumption, as indicated in Table 2-1, it meant that the mere threat of gas disruptions could be used as a significant instrument of coercion in combating Ukraine's new pro-Western attitudes.[70] In fact, Drezner named Ukraine "a primary candidate for Russian economic coercion,"[71] and my own *level of susceptibility to Russian coercion* formula, presented in Figure 2-4, also confirms this. This threat of coercion became even more potent when domestic instability was present,[72] as seen during the two winter Ukrainian "gas wars" of 2006 and 2009. It is no longer a secret that the 2006 and 2009 winter "Gas Wars"[73] were meant to suppress the popular support for Ukraine's Orange Revolution.[74] Clearly, an impartial analysis of the rise and fall of the Orange Revolution cannot be done without considering the merits of gas as an instrument of coercion. For Russia, the two gas disputes were a matter of both compellence and deterrence:[75]

- The Compellence Argument: The Russian use of economic statecraft was clearly meant to convince Ukraine to change its recalcitrant and independent behavior. The rise in the price of gas following the January 2006 crisis[76] resulted in the fall of Yushchenko`s government, led by Prime Minister Yuriy Yekhanurov.[77] This created a rift in the governing coalition and weakened the Orange Revolution.[78] Similarly, the January 2009 dispute resulted in the collapse of industry in Ukraine, and contributed to the shrinking of its economy by over 20 percent from 2008 to 2009—although certainly a large percentage of this estimate could be attributed to the great global recession.[79]
- Through these measures, Russia managed to send a clear, credible message to Ukraine: Europe and NATO are not viable alternatives to Russia.
- The Deterrence Argument: The threat of further gas disruptions deterred the Ukrainian voters, politicians, and even the government from continuing to support the Orange Revolution movement. Interestingly enough, the 2006 dispute took place just months before the parliamentary elections in Ukraine,[80] while the 2009 dispute took place just 1 year before the presidential elections in Ukraine. While Russia denied the fact that the gas disruptions were politically motivated,[81] and despite a lack of documentation to support the political implications of the two gas crises, it is hard to dismiss the psychological impact of a failed government and a failed economy over the electorate.[82] Russian interference in the affairs of Ukraine is also undeniable: Before the presidential elections, Rus-

sian President Medvedev publicly expressed hopes that the Ukrainian elections would bring "competent and effective authorities . . . open to the development of constructive, friendly, all-around relations with Russia."[83] Ultimately, by February 2010, the Orange Revolution was already considered "a thing of the past," or "officially over," with both Tymoshenko, a former supporter of the Orange revolution,[84] and Yanukovych taking pro-Russian stances.[85] After the defeat of the Orange Revolution in 2010, the foreign policy of Ukraine "seems to have realigned itself closer to the Russian Federation on a number of issues";[86] Ukrainian President Viktor Yanukovych described Russia as a "strategic partner, friendly and brotherly state."[87]

While the pro-Russian Yanukovych was willing to sellout "the strategic Sevastopol naval base in exchange for cash benefits for his oligarchic friends and supporters in the gas-trading and gas-consuming sectors,"[88] at least according to European political analysts, pro-NATO Yushchenko tried to portray himself as the reformist alternative. But his Orange Revolution was short-lived, because of Ukraine's dependence on Russian gas. A close look at Ukraine under the pro-NATO Viktor Yushchenko reveals that, in dealing with a noncooperating, even belligerent Ukraine, natural gas was an effective instrument of coercion in pursuing Russia's national security objectives at the Black Sea.

ENDNOTES - CHAPTER 3

1. Peter Zeihan, "Ukraine's Election and the Russian Resurgence," *STRATFOR*, January 26, 2010.

2. Richard Andres and Michael Kofman, "European Energy Security: Reducing Volatility of Ukraine-Russia Natural Gas Pricing Disputes," *INSS Strategic Forum*, No. 264, February 2011, p. 1.

3. Hrygoriy Perepelytsya, "Russia in State Policies of Ukraine," in Editura Cartea Veche, Gabi Radu, and Iulian Chifu, eds., *The Perception of Russia in Romania, Republic of Moldova, and Ukraine*, Bucharest, Romania: 2011, p. 371.

4. Volodymyr Horbach, "Modern Russia in the Ukrainian Public Sphere," Radu and Chifu, eds., p. 342.

5. *Ibid.*, p. 343.

6. Russia continues to exert today a great amount of psychological pressure on Ukrainian "media, business and political decisionmaking," but none of its pressures are as efficient instruments of coercion as is natural gas. Oleksandr Sushko, "Russian Economic Presence in Ukraine: Interests Evolution and Current Trends," Radu and Chifu, eds., p. 330.

7. Zbigniew Brzezinski, *Power and Principle: Memoirs of the National Security Adviser, 1977-1981*, New York: Farrar Straus & Giroux, 1990; Zbigniew Brzezinski, "The Premature Partnership," *Foreign Affairs*, Vol. 73, No. 2, March-April 1994, pp. 67-82.

8. Danylo Hawaleshka, "The Back-to-Moscow Election?" *Maclean's*, Vol. 123, No. 5, February 15, 2010, pp. 22-23.

9. Catherine Belton, Neil Buckley, and Roman Olearchyk, "Russia-Ukraine Gas Peace Threatens to Unravel," *Financial Times*, September 23, 2010.

10. Nadejda Victor and David G. Victor, "Bypassing Ukraine: Exporting Russian Gas to Poland and Germany," in *Natural Gas and Geopolitics from 1970 to 2040*, David G. Victor, Amy Jaffe, and Mark H. Hayes, eds., New York: Cambridge University Press, 2006, p. 164.

11. Steve Chan and Cooper Drury, "Sanctions as Economic Statecraft: An Overview," in *Sanctions as Economic Statecraft*, Steve Chan and Cooper Drury, eds., New York: St. Martin's Press, 2000, p. 1; Randall E. Newnham, "More Flies with Honey: Positive Economic Linkage in German Ostpolitik from Bismarck to Kohl," *International Studies Quarterly*, Vol. 44, No. 1, March 2000, p. 73.

12. Daniel Drezner, "The Complex Causation of Sanction Outcomes," in Chan and Drury, eds., p. 212.

13. Daniel Drezner, *The Sanctions Paradox. Economic Statecraft and International Relations*, New York: Cambridge University Press, 1999, p. 198.

14. This is a demand that in the case of Ukraine has not only geopolitical and economic considerations, but nationalistic ones: the Kremlin requiring recognition of Russia as the protector of Russians living in Ukraine—comprising 22 percent of Ukraine's population. Drezner, *The Complex Causation of Sanction Outcomes*, p. 222.

15. Mykola Riabchuk, a former Fulbright fellow and a senior research associate at the Ukrainian Centre for Cultural Studies, wrote that "in 1991, when the Soviet Union suddenly and dramatically collapsed, the country inherited 15 percent of the Soviet nuclear stockpile: some 130 liquid-fuel SS-19 missiles, each with six nuclear warheads; 46 solid-fuel SS-24 missiles, each with 10 warheads; and 44 *Tupolev*-95 and *Tupolev*-160 strategic bombers, with a total of 1,081 nuclear cruise missiles. Before it even had a constitution of its own, Ukraine possessed the third-largest nuclear arsenal in the world." Mykola Riabchuk, "Ukraine's Nuclear Nostalgia," *World Policy Journal*, Vol. 26, No. 4, Winter 2009, pp. 95-105.

16. Drezner, *The Sanctions Paradox*, p. 202.

17. Mykola Riabchuk, "Ukraine's Nuclear Nostalgia," *World Policy Journal*, Vol. 26, No. 4, Winter 2009, p. 99.

18. Drezner, *The Sanctions Paradox*, p. 199.

19. *Ibid.*

20. *Ibid.*, p. 200.

21. Riabchuk, pp. 95-105.

22. Drezner, *The Sanctions Paradox*, p. 202.

23. John J. Mearsheimer, "The Case for a Ukrainian Nuclear Deterrent," *Foreign Affairs*, Vol. 72, No. 3, Summer 1993, p. 53.

24. *Ibid.*, p. 55.

25. Drezner, *The Complex Causation of Sanction Outcomes*, p. 230.

26. George Lopez and David Cortright, "Assessing Smart Sanctions: Lessons from the 1990s," in *Smart Sanctions. Targeting Economic Statecraft*, George Lopez and David Cortright, eds., Lanham, MD: Rowman & Littlefield Publishers, Inc, 2002, p. 16.

27. Riabchuk, p. 99.

28. This unpopular move did indeed contribute to the low voter turnout in the 1994 parliamentary elections in Ukraine.

29. Drezner, *The Sanctions Paradox*, p. 53.

30. Hossein G. Askari *et al.*, *Economic Sanctions. Examining their Philosophy and Efficacy*, Westport, CT: Praeger, 2003, p. 123.

31. The costs of coercion was used to convince the Russian Duma to support the Government's plans for additional natural gas pipelines.

32. Victor and Victor, p. 145.

33. *Ibid.*, p. 123.

34. Jeffrey Mankoff, *Eurasian Energy Security*, Washington, DC: Council on Foreign Relations, 2009.

35. Gary C. Hufbauer, Jeffrey J. Schott, and Kimberly A. Elliott, *Economic Sanctions Reconsidered: History and Current Policy*, Second Ed., Washington, DC: Institute for International Economics, 1990, p. 41.

36. Alexander Bor, "Ukraine Seeks Changes in Terms of Russian Gas Accord," *Platts Oilgram News*, July 5, 2010, p. 7.

37. Zeyno Baran argued that "Moscow's entire energy strategy is predicated on continuing and expanding its dominant market position in Europe and Eurasia. This position can only be maintained if Russia holds a near monopoly on pipelines into Europe." Zeyno Baran, "EU Energy Security: Time to End Russian Leverage," *Washington Quarterly*, Vol. 30, No. 4, October 2007, p. 138.

38. Drezner, *The Sanctions Paradox*, p. 200.

39. *Ibid.*, p. 202.

40. *Ibid.*, p. 203.

41. Svetlana Stepanenko, "Ukrainian Foreign Minister Deplores Russian 'Blackmail' Over Gas Prices; Some in Ukraine Want to Invoke International Guarantees of its Security Pledged in 1994 when it Gave Up Nuclear Arms; Russian Navy Chief: Terms of Black Sea Fleet Basing," *Current Digest of the Post-Soviet Press*, Vol. 57, No. 51, January 18, 2006, pp. 7-8.

42. Drezner, *The Sanctions Paradox*, p. 204.

43. *Ibid.*, p. 205.

44. Bor, p. 7.

45. "Russia: Ukrainian Natural Gas Purchases Cut," *STRATFOR*, September 30, 2010.

46. It is widely acknowledged today that the drop in the price of Russian natural gas was the direct result of the April 2010 contentious "Kharkov Treaties," which allowed the stationing of Russia's Black Sea Fleet within Ukraine's borders. Christie, Baev, and Golovko.

47. Centre for European Policy Studies (CEPS), May 5, 2010.

48. Bor, p. 7.

49. Joanna Sopinska, "Eu/ Ukraine : Yanukovych Wins Praise for Energy Sector Reforms," *Europolitics Daily* (in English), September 15, 2010.

50. *Russia: Ukrainian Natural Gas Purchases Cut*, September 30, 2010.

51. "The Regulatory Effects of Russia and Ukraine's 'Gas War' are Emerging," *MarketWatch: Global Round-Up*, Vol. 8, No. 9, September 2009, p. 171.

52. Russia wants to control Ukraine's natural gas infrastructure not only to increase its coercive power over Ukraine and ensure that natural gas to Western Europe is not interrupted by Ukraine in the future, but also to make sure that Ukrainian pipelines are not being used by anyone else to redirect natural gas, in case Russia decides to stop the flow of natural gas to other ECE countries like Poland through the Yamal pipeline in the future.

53. Andres and Kofman, p. 2.

54. *Ibid.*, p. 2.

55. While during the 2009 Ukraine gas cutoff Russia moderately increased the delivery of natural gas supplies through the Yamal pipeline, many in the ECE and even Southern Germany were severely affected by the disruption of supplies. Christie, Baev, and Golovko.

56. Costis Geropoulos, "Putin to Ukraine: No Merger, no Gas Talks," *New Europe*, October 31, 2010.

57. Anders Aslund and Andrew Kuchins, *The Russia Balance Sheet*, Washington, DC: Peterson Institute for International Economics, Center for Strategic and International Studies, 2009, p. 62.

58. Marshall Goldman, *Petrostate. Putin, Power, and the New Russia*, New York: Oxford University Press, 2008, p. 142.

59. Belton, Buckley, and Olearchyk, p. 4.

60. "Bill Allowing Russia to Run Ukrainian Gas Pipes Coming Soon-Gazprom," *BBC Monitoring Kiev Unit Supplied by BBC Worldwide Monitoring*, September 24, 2010. That same month, Russia requested Ukraine to refuse transport of gas to Poland in an effort to leverage Poland's gas shortage to coerce the latter into giving up its rights to the Yamal-Europe gas pipeline until 2045. "Ukraine Suspends Gas Supply to Poland at Russia's Request," *BBC Monitoring Kiev Unit Supplied by BBC Worldwide Monitoring*, September 27, 2010.

61. "Government's Gas Counter-Offensive," *Polish News Bulletin,* September 23, 2010.

62. Geropoulos,.

63. "Russia/Ukraine: Putin's Gas-Merger Plan," *Business Eastern Europe*, Vol. 39, No. 16, May 3, 2010, pp. 1-2.

64. "Gazprom and Naftogaz Slow to Consolidate," *NEWSB-CM*, November 1, 2010.

65. "Ukraine Wants Naftogaz and Gazprom Joint Venture Soon Says PM," *RIA Novosti-Kiev*, April 12, 2011.

66. This was emphasized also by Richard Andres, who predicts that "it is doubtful that Ukraine can continue timely payments for its domestic gas consumption and maintain its own pipeline infrastructure. Fundamental changes to Russia-Ukraine energy transport agreements are coming." Andres and Kofman, p. 1.

67. Mearsheimer, 55.

68. Goldman, p. 144.

69. Edward Lucas, *The New Cold War: Putin's Russia and the Threat to the West,* New York: Palgrave MacMillan, 2009, p. 145.

70. Drezner, *The Complex Causation of Sanction Outcomes*, p. 224.

71. Drezner, *The Sanctions Paradox*, p. 207.

72. Drezner, *The Complex Causation of Sanction Outcomes*, p. 229.

73. *Gas Wars*, Vol. 390, *Economist Newspaper Limited*, 2009, p. 12-12.

74. "The Winter Gas War," *Wall Street Journal-Eastern Edition*, Vol. 253, No. 5, January 7, 2009, p. A12.

75. Hufbauer, Schott, and Elliott, p. 11.

76. "Putin's Gas Squeeze," *Wall Street Journal-Eastern Edition*, Vol. 247, No. 1, January 3, 2006, p. A24.

77. "Gas Deal Brings Down Yushchenko`s Government," *Current Digest of the Post-Soviet Press*, Vol. 58, No. 1, February, 2006, pp. 5-16.

78. "Gas Poisoning," *Country Monitor*, Vol. 14, No. 2, January 16, 2006, p. 4-4.

79. *The Regulatory Effects of Russia and Ukraine's 'Gas War' are Emerging*, p. 171.

80. *Gas Poisoning*, p. 4-4.

81. Goldman, p. 145.

82. Hufbauer, Schott, and Elliott, p. 11. Russian analysts, together with the opposition in Ukraine, argued that the decrease in the standards of living and the reduction of income were solely the result of bad management of the economy by the leadership of the Orange Revolution. However, let us consider the facts: Between 2005 and 2009--basically, for the duration of Ukraine's Orange Revolution--the price or Russian natural gas experienced a fivefold price increase, in a country where 40 percent of total goods exports came from Ukrainian iron and steel during the

same period--commodities whose manufacturing depends on cheap natural gas. While conservative estimates indicate that this price increase represented less than 2 percent of Ukraine's gross domestic product (GDP) during that period, one must also consider that these measures were taken during a global economic crisis. Also, this 2 percent represents the costs of the energy price increase alone, and completely disregards the secondary effects the price increase had on the Ukrainian industry as a whole; and does not account for the costs to the Ukrainian economy of the 2006 and 2009 gas cuts, either. Edward Christie, Pavel Baev, and Volodymyr Golovko, "Vulnerability and Bargaining Power in EU-Russia Gas Relations," *FIW-Research Reports 2010/11*, No. 3, March 2011, pp. 23-27.

83. Richard Bourdeaux, "Kremlin Ends Freeze with Kiev, in Relief Over Election," *Wall Street Journal-Eastern Edition*, Vol. 255, No. 20, January 26, 2010, p. A11.

84. "A Storm is Brewing in the East Despite Temporary Gas Truce," *MarketWatch: Energy*, Vol. 5, No. 8, August, 2006, pp. 19-21.

85. Hawaleshka, pp. 22-23.

86. Christie, Baev, and Golovko.

87. Perepelytsya, p. 373.

88. Michael Emerson, "President Yanukovich's Dubious Deal," *EU Neighbourhood Policy, CEPS Commentaries*, May 5, 2010.

CHAPTER 4

DIVIDE UT REGNES:
REFLEXIVE CONTROL AND GAS PIPELINE
POLITICS IN EURASIA

Russia's gas companies pursue strategies that make
little economic sense but that serve the long-term interests of the Russian state, namely, ensuring European
dependence on Russian energy supplies. For example,
Russia's undersea Nord Stream pipeline will cost at
least three times more than a proposed overland route
through Lithuania and Poland would have.[1]

Zeyno Baran

In the contemporary security environment, Russia
can no longer impose its will through the use of coercive military means against Western allies, as was the
case in Soviet times, and particularly during the Cold
War.[2] While the grand strategic ends of the Russian
foreign policy remain fundamentally the same, after
Putin's *Russia at the Turn of the Millennium* speech in
1999, "Russia modified the methods of pursuing its
foreign-policy objectives."[3] Indeed, explained Edward
Lucas, while the Old Cold War was fought with tanks
and missiles, the New Cold War "is fought with cash,
natural resources, diplomacy, and propaganda."[4] All
of these are tools of foreign policy that cannot be divorced from the natural gas pipeline politics of Eurasia,
and they are brought together by a concept known by
the Russian intelligentsia as "Reflexive Control" (RC).
It was mentioned in Chapter 2 that the bigger half
of the Russian territory lies east of the Urals on the
Asian continent, and that much of the Russian political elite agrees with former Russian Foreign Minister

Andrei Kozyrev that Russian "traditions come mostly, if not altogether, from Asia."[5] Not surprisingly, in accordance with Sun Tzu's adage that the best stratagem is the one that attacks the enemy's strategy, RC was developed by the Russians almost half a century ago as a means to interfere with the decisionmaking process of an opponent or a partner in support of Russia's grand strategic ends. Timothy Thomas defined RC as "the means of conveying to a partner or an opponent specially prepared information to incline him to voluntarily make the predetermined decision desired by the initiator of the action."[6] This chapter takes a quick look into RC as "the Soviet concept of influencing an adversary's decisionmaking process,"[7] and its use in the region's gas pipeline politics to bribe Western Europe, to divide the members of the North Atlantic Treaty Organization (NATO) and the European Union (EU), and to rule the Eastern and Central European (ECE) states.

It is no secret that the Russians employ reflexive control at "the strategic level in association with internal and external politics . . . as a method for achieving geopolitical superiority."[8] While much was written on the military uses of reflexive control, little attention was given to its use in international relations, despite the fact that "Russia's political elite also employs RC in analytical methodologies used to assess contemporary situations," and despite the fact that "when making decisions, the Kremlin pays attention to reflexive processes."[9]

A *reflex* is meant to cause the adversary to "make a decision unfavorable to himself."[10] This chapter attempts to reveal how Russia uses natural gas as an instrument to apply *power pressure* — a significant component of reflexive control — in order to divide its

Western neighbors and rule over its sphere of influence. To achieve these ends, Russia will continue to focus on bilateral economic deals that favor individual Western European states—like Germany, France, and Italy, the so-called center of the EU—in order to divide them politically from ECE countries—the periphery of the union and, as we have seen in Chapter 2, part of Russia's sphere of influence.[11] My argument here is that while Europe's center is able to achieve short-term economic interests from its dealings with Russia in the field of natural gas, at the detriment of the periphery, these gains will translate into long-term political loss for both the European center and its periphery, and into a geopolitical win for Russia. Russia is willing to incur a short-term economic loss as long as its long-term grand-strategic ends in its western sphere of influence are achieved.

REFLEXIVE CONTROL AGAINST NATO AND THE EUROPEAN UNION: BRIBE THE CENTER, DIVIDE THE UNION AND RULE ITS PERIPHERY[12]

Putin wrote in his Ph.D. dissertation that the primary focus of his study is an in-depth analysis of "the principles and mechanisms responsible for the formation of strategic systems used in strategic-planning," and their use to control the use of natural resources.[13] Putin defined strategic planning as "deliberate planning reforms based on prediction, managing and adapting expectations to achieve strategic objectives."[14] He emphasized that the strategic planning of Russia's natural resources must remain part of an "ordered, controlled, and integrated set"[15] of strategic decisions that are generated to support the greater national interests of Russia. A student of RC during his years in the KGB (the Russian security agency), Putin hinted in his dissertation, even though he never named the concept directly, that RC must become an integral part of Russia's grand strategy. He also hinted that the management of Russia's natural resources is a matter of the state, for the interests of the state, and not those of private entities.

Throughout history, Russia has used various tactics in order to ensure its survival and its status as a great power in Europe. During the Cold War, however, the means used in imposing the Soviet ends evolved, giving birth to what is known today as RC, or the concept of manipulating the decisionmaking process of both one's enemies and allies for the interest of the state.[16] While this concept can easily be confused with that of realpolitik—politics based primarily on practical and material factors and considerations—it differs from it in that RC allows for short-term material/economic loss on condition that long-term grand strategic political gains are achieved.

Russian military scholar Major General (Ret.) M. D. Ionov identified four basic methods for applying the concept of RC: (1) power pressure; (2) presenting false information about the situation (deception); (3) influencing the enemy's decisionmaking algorithm (attacking the enemy's strategy); and, (4) altering the decisionmaking time. In his essay about RC, Timothy Thomas focused on the last three methods, ignoring perhaps the most effective method of all, which includes the use of "ultimatums, threats of sanctions, and threats of risk."[17] This chapter suggests that Russia blends economic threats with incentives to achieve its political grand strategic ends, as seen in its relations with Ukraine, and that natural gas plays a central role in Russia's strategy against NATO and the EU.

British foreign policy thinker Mark Leonard defined power as the ability of a nation to achieve its grand strategic ends; he emphasized that Russia's power is growing because of its proven ability and willingness to use its natural resources, particularly its monopoly on natural gas, to weaken the EU.[18] By pursuing ancient Roman strategies, such as *divide ut regnes* (divide and rule), Russia is able to use its monopoly of the natural gas pipeline infrastructure to Europe to secure bilateral deals with individual member states, particularly Western states, to the detriment of the EU, although mostly to the detriment of Eastern and Central Europe.[19] States such as Germany, Italy, and France reflexively engage in this behavior in pursuit of their own short-term economic interests, leaving their eastern neighbors at the mercy of the "predatory nature"[20] of the Russian state, ultimately weakening the entire Union politically in the long term:

> Today, Berlin, Rome, and Paris show greater reluctance to pursue any alliance policy strongly opposed by Moscow. In addition, U.S. support for greater diversification of energy supplies for the more vulnerable countries of Eastern and Central Europe has been undercut by resistance from major Western European states. More important than European energy solidarity is their hope for a larger financial stake in energy projects promoted by Russia. These ventures may only increase Europe's vulnerabilities.[21]

Two such projects are the Nord Stream and South Stream natural gas pipelines. Nord Stream is a €10-15 billion Russia-controlled joint venture between Russia, Germany, and the Netherlands;[22] South Stream is a €12.8 billion Russia-controlled joint venture between Russia and Italy.[23] The two projects alone are expected to transform political relations in Europe, dividing the East from the West not only in the field of natural gas, but geopolitically as well. This is, however, not a diabolical Russian plot to tear the EU limb from limb,[24] but an attempt typical of the Soviet Union during the traditional security environment: to divide and weaken its neighbors in order to ensure its geopolitical supremacy.

While the Russian political elite claims that bilateral relations are not meant to divide the Union's center from its periphery, facts show otherwise. Konstantin Kosachev, Chairman of the Russian Duma Committee on Foreign Affairs and a member of Prime Minister Putin's United Russia Party, vows that this decision is purely bureaucratic in nature: "We are sick and tired of dealing with Brussels bureaucrats. In Germany, Italy, [and] France, we can achieve much more. The EU is not an institution that contributes to our relationship, but an institution that slows down progress."[25] Valery Vorobiev, Prorector of the Moscow State Institute of International Relations, even emphasized that the Lisbon Treaty "opened a new page [for NATO member states and Russia] in moving towards a common foreign policy."[26] In Chapter 2, I have shown, however, that this strategy is meant to undermine NATO and the power of the EU; and to a certain extent, Russia has already managed to do just that. Edward Lucas blames this development on "the gullibility and lack of imagination of all too many Western leaders,"[27] who fail to realize that Russia has not given up on its alleged right to control its sphere of influence. Whereas the relations between the center and the periphery of the EU are beset by national disagreements and bureaucratic impediments, the relationship between the center and Russia focuses primarily on natural gas, an area where Russia has the upper hand, particularly in ECE. Mark Leonard argued that "this has allowed Russia to maximize its influence over the Union, while the EU has been less able to capitalize on its potential to influence Russia. In short, Russia has transformed its weakness into power, while Europe's power has been turned into weakness."[28] Leonard further emphasized that this is particularly astounding, given the power of the EU as a united geo-economic body:

> What makes Russia's ascendance so surprising is that on almost all indicators of power — soft and hard — the European Union continues to outrank Russia, by some measures even more than in the 1990s. The EU's combined economy is almost 15 times the size of Russia's. Even with all the oil wealth, Russia's GDP is barely as big as Belgium's and the Netherlands' combined. The EU's population is three and a half times the size of Russia's; its military spending is seven times bigger; the EU has five seats on the UN Security Council (of which two are permanent) to Russia's one.[29]

This radical shift from a position of power to one of weakness has been made possible particularly due to the EU failure to advance a common energy policy that encourages energy diversification, especially in ECE countries that depend heavily on Russian natural gas. Instead, Old Member States continue to "intertwine their rational self-interests vis-à-vis the EU (i.e, against supranationalism) with that vis-à-vis third parties, including negotiations with Russia";[30] even by encouraging economically unprofitable projects for Russia. However, that approach further subjugates ECE to Russia: "as such, Russia has partnered with Germany to build Nord Stream and with Italy to build South Stream pipelines to control the flow of Russian and Central European energy supply to Western Europe."[31] Not surprisingly, since Germany and Italy are the top two importers of Russian natural gas, the Nord Stream and South Stream gas pipeline projects were supported by many officials who benefited from their "financial ties to Russia's Gazprom, thereby furthering European acceptance of Moscow's pipeline projects."[32]

But these divisions between the center and the periphery of the EU—between Old and New Europe—are anything but new; they originate in both the history and the geography of the Eurasian supercontinent. Nations like Germany and France have historically carried out bilateral relations with Russia on an equal footing, while conducting business with the countries in between from a position of superiority. Diana Bozhilova, a post-doctoral research fellow at the London School of Economics, asserts that this type of relationship at different echelons continues today; and it is justified by the fact that the EU's center perceives that in successfully dealing with Russia in the past, it has much more experience than the Eastern and Central European countries:

> Old Europe . . . is relatively more experienced with international high politics through the conduct of two world wars. Moreover, there exists historical elements of equality in the internationalization of their respective relationships with both the former USSR [Union of Soviet Socialist Republics] and Russia throughout much of the twentieth century. As a result, their "knowledge" of and experience with bilateral relations with Russia is invariably greater than that occurring between the CEECs [Central and Eastern European Countries] and Russia.[33]

108

Both Russia and the European center continue to see international politics as "a series of tête-à-têtes between great powers,"[34] seducing each other with economic incentives, in spite of the political consequences to the countries in between, which more often than not are viewed as "costly distractions."[35] This is particularly true in Russia's relationship with Germany. In fact, it could be argued that the emergence of Russia as a more assertive player in international relations coincided with the improved dynamics in the political and economic relations between the two nations.[36]

Despite two world wars fought between the two nations, Russia's special relationship with Germany dates back to 18th century's Catherine the Great, when the latter allowed German nobles to control the Baltic provinces and encouraged German farmers to inhabit the Volga basin.[37] Economic and political ties continued to be strong in prerevolutionary Russia, when royal families intermarried, and Germany invested a lot of capital in Russia. This historic relationship has been renewed after Germany's reunification, particularly due to an increased dependency on Russian natural gas. (In Soviet times, East Germany imported most if not all of its natural gas from the Soviet Union.)

More recently, collaboration on projects such as the building of Russia's Nord Stream gas pipeline beneath the Baltic Sea to Germany, a pipeline that is meant to bypass Poland and Ukraine and thus decrease their geostrategic influence, further emphasizes that Germany places its relationship with Russia before its relations with other ECE countries. Former German Chancellor Schröder, whom Moscow recruited as the chief executive officer of Nord Stream by paying him a substantial salary,[38] personally championed the newly founded Russo-German alliance by testifying that

Germany "must be a partner of Russia if we want to share in the vast raw material reserves in Siberia. The alternative for Russia would be to share these reserves with China."[39] Radek Sikorski, currently the Minister of Foreign Affairs of Poland, previously compared the new Russo-German alliance and the Nord Stream project to the Molotov-Ribbentrop Pact, also known as the Treaty of Non-Aggression between Nazi Germany and the Soviet Union. In 1939, the Molotov-Ribbentrop Pact divided ECE into Soviet and German spheres of influence, including geographically dividing Poland between the two countries.[40]

In its relations with Germany, the Russian leadership, particularly, Putin, proved to be a master of perceptions. He convinced the Germans that Russia is a reformed regional power and a credible European partner (effectively changing the narrative/rhetoric in the German public sphere from Russia as the antagonist threat, to Russia as the protagonist partner). Russian President Medvedev declared that "the highly efficient cooperation between Russia and Germany in the international arena, which come to . . . the strengthening of global and regional stability and security."[41] Yet, throughout the EU, this cognitive dissonance with regard to Russia is very much alive. While Putin provided economic incentives to Germany by opening his country's market to German companies like; DaimlerChrysler, BMW, Deutsche Bank, etc, at the same time he took advantage of this friendship to increase his grasp over the ECE natural gas market.[42] And with Germany remaining Russia's largest market for gas (which will continue to be the case, now that Germany will shut all its nuclear reactors by 2022 in a reaction to the Fukushima disaster), it is unlikely that Germany will forgo Russia's economic incentives for the sake of ECE—even though in the long term this economic alliance will cause NATO's and the EU's political disunity.[43] Indeed, the lack of political agreement between the Old and New Europe, particularly in the natural gas field, means that Russia "increasingly defines the rules of the game";[44] and many ECE states already realize that "they cannot count on EU support when Russia uses economic coercion against them."[45]

Improvements in Russo-German relations have been followed by an improvement in the relations between Russia and France. The sale by France, a NATO member state, of several *Mistral* class warships to Russia[46] over the past couple of years also gave birth to a strong Franco-Russian alliance that is best described through the prophetic words of Charles de Gaulle: "[F]or France and Russia to be united means being strong, being separated means being in danger. Indeed, this is an immutable condition from the viewpoint of geographical location, experience and common sense."[47] Ironically, the French position has been that "close ties with Russia can be regarded not only as a means of augmenting the power of France within the European Union but also the power of Europe itself."[48] Marina Arzakanyan, Chief Researcher at the Institute of World History, and Tatyana Zvereva, Senior Fellow at the Institute for Contemporary International Studies, explained that this close relationship persuaded the two nations to dedicate the names of the year 2010 to each other:

> At the end of the 20th and beginning of the 21st centuries, Russian-French relations with their long traditions became a strong monolith of political economic scientific educational literary and art affairs. The two states have entered a stage of privileged partnership. This prompted the governments of both countries to

declare 2010 the Year of Russia in France and the Year of France in Russia.[49]

To make matters worse, 2010 also marked the renewal in trilateral format of the France-Germany-Russia Summit, when Presidents Sarkozy, Medvedev, and Chancellor Merkel met in Deauville, France, and "compared notes on the main issues of international and European security on the eve of the NATO summit."[50] Jean-Louis Gergorin, cofounder and former Director of the Policy Planning Staff of the French Foreign Ministry who currently lectures at the *Institut d'Études Politiques de Paris*, emphasized that the tripartite[51] meeting in Deauville represents the birth of a new Franco-German-Russian triangle,[52] and from the political discourse in the three countries, it is likely that this alliance will take precedence over the greater interests of the NATO alliance.

But Europe's core alone cannot be blamed for Europe's divisions. Russia used similar RC strategies like it used in Germany and France in its natural gas negotiations with nearly every European nation. Mark Leonard argues that European Member States are already divided over their relationship with Russia, and Russia is already slowly emerging as the victor in its relations with Europe. To prove this point, Leonard divided the European Member States into five categories that differentiate each country's partnership with Russia, particularly with regard to European policies: Trojan Horses, Strategic Partners, Friendly Pragmatists, Frosty Pragmatists, and New Cold Warriors:

> "Trojan Horses" (Cyprus and Greece) who often defend Russian interests in the EU system, and are willing to veto common EU positions; "Strategic Partners" (France, Germany, Italy, and Spain) who enjoy a

"special relationship" with Russia which occasionally undermines common EU policies; "Friendly Pragmatists" (Austria, Belgium, Bulgaria, Finland, Hungary, Luxembourg, Malta, Portugal, Slovakia, and Slovenia) who maintain a close relationship with Russia and tend to put their business interests above political goals; "Frosty Pragmatists" (Czech Republic, Denmark, Estonia, Ireland, Latvia, the Netherlands, Romania, Sweden, and the United Kingdom) who also focus on business interests but are less afraid than others to speak out against Russian behaviour on human rights or other issues; and "New Cold Warriors" (Lithuania and Poland) who have an overtly hostile relationship with Moscow and are willing to use the veto to block EU negotiations with Russia.[53]

While Europe's core will continue to enjoy the benefits of good economic relations with Putin's Russia,[54] by signing long-term deals in the field of natural gas at the expense of the periphery,[55] "the countries in between";[56] the former ought to be reminded that Putin himself is keen on alluding to the Russian proverb: "friendship is friendship, but to each his own tobacco."[57] In other words, despite the economic partnership between the European center and Russia, the former must understand that economic alliances will only go as far as they contribute to Russia's political grand strategic goals which, as we have seen in Chapter 2, depend on the weakening of NATO's geo-strategic power, and on Russia's control over its traditional sphere of influence.[58]

	EU	NATO
Austria	YES	NO
Belgium	YES	YES
Bulgaria	YES	YES
Cyprus	YES	NO
Czech Republic	YES	YES
Denmark	YES	YES
Estonia	YES	YES
Finland	YES	NO
France	YES	YES
Germany	YES	YES
Greece	YES	YES
Hungary	YES	YES
Ireland	YES	NO
Italy	YES	YES
Latvia	YES	YES
Lithuania	YES	YES
Luxembourg	YES	YES
Malta	YES	NO
Netherlands	YES	YES
Norway	NO	YES
Poland	YES	YES
Portugal	YES	YES
Romania	YES	YES
Slovakia	YES	YES
Slovenia	YES	YES
Spain	YES	YES
Sweden	YES	NO
United Kingdom	YES	YES

Source: author's representation.

Table 4-1. Membership of European Nations in EU and/or NATO.

AU REVOIR NATO CONSENSUS: HOW NORD STREAM AND SOUTH STREAM WILL TRANSFORM THE CONTEMPORARY SECURITY ENVIRONMENT IN EUROPE

The fear of many policymakers, including Zbigniew Brzezinski[59] and Senator Richard Lugar, is that European divisions in the field of natural gas between

Old Europe and New Europe can and will ultimately express themselves geopolitically in divisions among NATO's old and new members. These divisions are amplified by the unwillingness of many ECE countries to oppose Russia because of fear that Russia will use its monopoly of natural gas to ECE as an instrument of coercion that could slow economic growth, but also by the reluctance of many Western European countries to oppose Russia politically, for fear of losing the short-term economic benefits that Russia bribes them with. This being said, Germany, despite being the least European NATO member susceptible to Russian coercion, as shown in Chapter 1, will still support Russia's policies as long as the short-term economic gains are ensured. In fact, because of the growing intensification of economic ties between Germany and Russia, Stephen Larrabee also expects that "Berlin is going to react cautiously to proposals that could lead to a deterioration of relations with Moscow. This will make the pursuit of a coherent transatlantic policy toward Russia much more difficult in the future."[60] Evidence of this is the recent UN Resolution 1973 (2011), which authorized NATO "to take all necessary measures . . . to protect civilians and civilian populated areas under threat of attack in the Libyan Arab Jamahiriya, including Benghazi."[61] The Resolution was adopted by a vote of 10 in favor to none against, with five abstentions: the BRIC countries (Brazil, Russia, India, China) plus Germany.[62]

But this economic relationship between Russia and Europe's core does not diminish the importance of natural gas as an instrument of coercion. As we have seen in the data presented at the end of Chapter 1, the degree of dependence on Russian natural gas varies considerably among EU and NATO member states—with many ECE states completely dependent on Russian natural gas.[63] That means that aside from Europe's center, its periphery may ultimately be NATO's downfall, because while Germany is unwilling to forgo the economic benefits it receives from Russia, a change in this policy will not cause the collapse of the German economy. However, if ECE countries like Bulgaria were to oppose Russia's foreign policy objectives, a Russian natural gas embargo would collapse their economy within months rather than years—as illustrated also in Chapter 1 by the secondary effects of the Ukrainian 2009 affair on the Bulgarian economy.

This becomes problematic for the North Atlantic Alliance, particularly when we consider that "all NATO decisions are made by consensus . . . that has been accepted as the sole basis for decisionmaking in NATO since the creation of the Alliance in 1949."[64] Since it takes only one out of 28 NATO member countries to influence NATO's decisionmaking process, and because many members' economies depend on Russian natural gas, Russia can rest assured that NATO will not be able to adopt policies that will negatively affect Russia's grand strategic interests. This is yet another reason why Russia must maintain a monopoly over the natural gas going to ECE, as was illustrated in the Ukraine case.

While many European and American policymakers see the problem, they are not willing to risk their political careers to take on a fight that is considered by many as "existentialist."[65] Ultimately, nothing will stop German, French, and Italian companies "from doing their own deals with Gazprom";[66] and without a common European energy strategy, nothing will stop Russia from controlling the flow of natural gas through its perceived sphere of influence. In fact, Russia's deals with Europe's center, particularly with regard to the Nord Stream and South Stream projects, will further ensure Russia's monopoly of natural gas to ECE. As Edward Lucas explains it, "so far, the stage has been set perfectly for the Kremlin's favorite tactic: divide and rule. Its success can be seen most clearly in the tale of two pipelines."[67]

In this Russian stratagem, both the Nord Stream and South Stream natural gas pipelines are instruments of Russian state power that will decrease the geostrategic importance of many ECE NATO member states as transit countries for Russian natural gas to the West. By circumventing many ECE countries (see Figure 4-1), the two pipelines will allow Russia to better employ natural gas as an instrument of coercion in its sphere of influence, Europe's eastern periphery, without attracting the criticism of Europe's core— Germany, France, and Italy.[68] This is particularly obvious in the case of Nord Stream,[69] the undersea section of which was scheduled to be completed in mid-May 2011. This will not only isolate Ukraine further from Europe, but will also increase Russia's influence over Poland, Slovakia, and the Czech Republic, which so far have successfully used their attributes as natural gas transit states to protect themselves against Russia politically.

> Stream's advantage for the Kremlin is clear. Russia's two existing gas export pipelines to Germany go across other countries — Belarus and Poland in the north, and Ukraine, Slovakia and the Czech Republic to the south. That means that deliveries to Germany are hostage to those transit countries' good will; put another way, if the Kremlin tries to punish those countries, it's more important customers further west may suffer.[70]

117

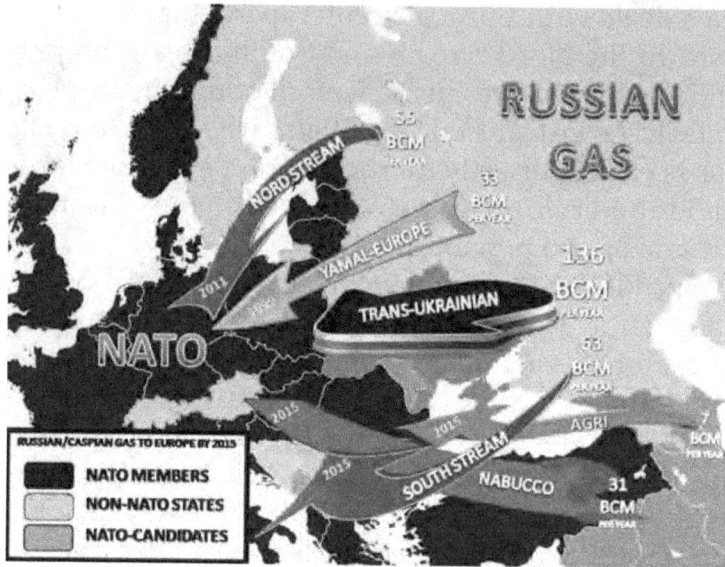

Source: author's representation.

Figure 4-1. Graphical Representation
of European Natural Gas Pipeline Politics.

Furthermore, Russia used Nord Stream as a "cata-lyst for increased Russian military presence and intel-ligence surveillance,"[71] being protected by the Russian Baltic Sea Navy, whose new role gave Russia "an intelligence edge in the Baltic Sea concerning all air, surface, and sub-surface activities—especially around Estonia, Finland, Sweden, and Denmark, and NATO members' military exercises."[72] Disturbingly enough, the project was supported by Germany, despite the dangers it represents for NATO, and even for Ger-many's long term political interests in the European Union:[73]

Nord Stream is the child of the most notorious diplomatic alliance in Europe's modern history, between the previous German government headed by former chancellor Gerhard Schroeder and Putin's Kremlin. It was blessed with a secret €1 billion loan guarantee issued just days before the German leader left office—shortly to become the chairman of the pipeline consortium.[74]

The strategic narrative with regard to Russia depends on how Russia uses natural gas to shape European politics: By combining calculated decisionmaking methodologies (through the use of RC) with the power to inflict severe economic harm or to provide incentives through the monopoly on gas supplies, Russia is able to use the Caspian and Russian gas pipelines to Europe to act either as "umbilical cords,"[75] whose disruption would prove devastating to any belligerent state's economy, or as pots of honey for energy-hungry friendly nations. Ultimately, controlling the decisionmaking process in individual EU Member States through power pressure in the context of natural gas negotiations is reflexive control at its best. This proves that traditional tools of influence are still very much relevant in the contemporary security environment, and in Russia's ability to weaken the NATO alliance.[76]

ENDNOTES - CHAPTER 4

1. Zeyno Baran, "EU Energy Security: Time to End Russian Leverage," *Washington Quarterly*, Vol. 30, No. 4, October 2007, p. 135.

2. Christian Thorun, *Explaining Change in Russian Foreign Policy: The Role of Ideas in Post-Soviet Russia's Conduct Towards the West*, New York: Palgrave MacMillan, 2009, p. 33.

3. Andrei Tsygankov, "Russia's Foreign Policy," in *After Putin's Russia: Past Imperfect, Future Uncertain*, 4th Ed, Stephen K. Wegren and Dale R. Herspring, eds., Plymouth, UK: Rowman & Littlefield Publishers, Inc, 2010, p. 225.

4. Edward Lucas, *The New Cold War: Putin's Russia and the Threat to the West*, New York: Palgrave MacMillan, 2009, p. 10.

5. Jerrold Schecter, *Russian Negotiating Behavior*, Washington, DC: United States Institute of Peace Press, 1998, p. 49.

6. Timothy L. Thomas, "Russia's Reflexive Control Theory and the Military," *Journal of Slavic Military Studies*, Vol. 17, No. 2, April, 2004, p. 240.

7. Vladimir Lefebvre and Victorina Lefebvre, "Reflexive Control: The Soviet Concept of Influencing an Adversary's Decision-making Process," Englewood, CO: SAIC, 1984.

8. Thomas, p. 240.

9. *Ibid.*, p. 241.

10. *Ibid.*

11. Edward Lucas identified this sphere of influence as "the countries bordering Russia, starting with those covered by the 1939 Molotov-Ribbentrop pact—the Baltic States, Central Europe, and the Balkans—but reaching around the Black Sea to the Caucasus." This, he argued, is the main theater of the New Cold War, Lucas, p. 10.

12. Edward Lucas wrote that "in the coming years, Europe will experience growing dependence on scanty and expensive Russian gas, with little chance of alternative supplies. Russia wields the energy weapon to bully its enemies and bribe its allies, and uses its financial clout to buy friends and influence." Lucas, p. 11.

13. Vladimir Vladimirovich Putin, "The Strategic Planning of Regional Natural Resources Under the Formation of Market Relations," Ph. D. Thesis in Economics, Saint Petersburg State Mining University, pp. 1-218.

14. *Ibid.*

15. *Ibid.*

16. Lefebvre and Lefebvre, p. 4.

17. Thomas, p. 244.

18. Mark Leonard and Nicu Popescu, *A Power Audit of EU-Russia Relations*, Cambridge Grove, London, UK: European Council on Foreign Relations, 2007.

19. Baran, p. 131.

20. Lucas, p. xii.

21. Keith Smith, *Russia-Europe Energy Relations: Implications for U.S. Policy*, Washington DC: CSIS, 2010.

22. Christina Lin, *The Prince of Rosh: Russian Energy Imperialism and the Emerging Eurasian Military Alliance of the Shanghai Cooperation Organization,* Berlin, Germany: Institute for Strategic-Political-Security-and Economic Consultancy (ISPSW), 2009.

23. *Ibid.*

24. Leonard and Popescu, p. 14.

25. *Ibid.*

26. "Russia and France: A New Quality of Relations," *International Affairs*, Vol. 57, No. 1, 2011, p. 37.

27. Lucas, p. xii.

28. Leonard and Popescu, p. 10.

29. *Ibid.*

30. Diana Bozhilova and Tom Hashimoto, "EU-Russia Energy Negotiations: A Choice between Rational Self-Interest and Collective Action," *European Security*, Vol. 19, No. 4, December 2010, p. 630.

31. Lin, p. 4.

32. Smith, p. 4.

33. Bozhilova and Hashimoto, p. 630.

34. Leonard and Popescu, p. 14.

35. Lucas, p. 158.

36. Stephen F. Larrabee, "Russia, Ukraine, and Central Europe: The Return of Geopolitics," *Journal of International Affairs*, Vol. 63, No. 2, Spring, 2010, p. 46.

37. Lucas, p. 171.

38. Smith, p. 4.

39. Daniel Freifeld, "The Great Pipeline Opera," *Foreign Policy*, No. 174, September 2009, p. 123.

40. Larrabee, p. 47.

41. Nikolai Pavlov, "Twenty Years of German Unity," *International Affairs*, Vol. 57, No. 1, 2011, p. 84.

42. Matthew Clements, ed., *Country Risk Assessments: Russia and the CIS*, 24th Ed., Alexandria, VA: *Jane's Sentinel*, 2009, p. 485.

43. Larrabee, p. 47.

44. Leonard and Popescu, p. 7.

45. Smith, p. 7.

46. "Russia and France: A New Quality of Relations," *International Affairs*, Vol. 57, No. 1, 2011, p. 32.

47. Marina Arzakanyan and Tatyana Zvereva, "Three Hundred Years of Cooperation," *International Affairs*, Vol. 57, No. 1, 2011, pp. 12-21.

48. "Russia and France: A New Quality of Relations," *International Affairs*, p. 23.

49. Arzakanyan and Zvereva, pp. 12-21.

50. *Ibid.*

51. "Russia and France: A New Quality of Relations," p. 23.

52. *Ibid.*, p. 32.

53. Leonard and Popescu, p. 2.

54. In fact, shortly after President Medvedev himself insisted that "there is a need to intensify cooperation between France, Germany, and Italy," Sergei Vasiliev, Deputy Director of the International Institute of Energy Policy and Diplomacy at the Moscow State Institute of International Relations, was proud to announce that three joint institutes that focus on European energy security had been established by the renowned diplomatic school of the Ministry of Foreign Affairs of Russia: the Russian-German Institute of Energy Policy and Economics; the Russian-Italian Institute of International Energy Studies, and the Russian and French Institute of Energy Diplomacy. "Russia and France: A New Quality of Relations," p. 37; Armen Oganesyan, "Energy Industry and Ecology," *International Affairs*, Vol. 57, No. 1, 2011, p. 228.

55. *Ibid.*

56. Lucas, p. 158.

57. Minton Goldman, ed., *Russia. the Eurasian Republics, and Central/Eastern Europe*, 10th Ed., Dubuque, IA: Global Studies, 2005, p. 112.

58. While an argument can be made that NATO and the European Union are two different bodies, and that affairs within the European Union will not impact the effective power of NATO, the reality shows otherwise. Divisions within Europe will in fact result in divisions within NATO, as Table 4-1 clearly indicates.

59. Zbigniew Brzezinski wrote that:

Russia is not an enemy, but it still views NATO with hostility. That hostility is not likely to fade soon, especially if Prime Minister Vladimir Putin becomes president again in 2012. Moreover, for a while yet, Russia's policy toward NATO, driven by historical resentment of the Soviet defeat in the Cold War and by nationalist hostility to NATO's expansion, is likely to try to promote division between the United States and Europe and, within Europe, between NATO's old members and NATO's new members.

Zbigniew Brzezinski, "An Agenda for NATO," *Foreign Affairs*, Vol. 88, No. 5, September 2009, pp. 2-20.

60. Larrabee, p. 48.

61. *United Nations Security Council Resolution*, Public Law 1973, 2011.

62. While purely symbolic, Germany's vote on the UN Resolution 1973 illustrates best Germany's foreign policy move away from its alliances in the traditional security environment and away from its fellow NATO member states, and closer to markets it perceives to have more economic potential, such as Russia and China.

63. Virginia Comolli, "Energy Security," in Bastian Giegerich, ed., *Europe and Global Security,* London, UK: International Institute for Strategic Studies, 2010, p. 188.

64. Brzezinski, pp. 2-20.

65. According to Marik String, this is how the topic was addressed in Brussels when Senator Lugar approached it. Interview conducted by the author with Marik String, Professional Staff Member for European and Eurasian Affairs, Committee on Foreign Relations, Washington, DC, February 9, 2011.

66. Lucas p. 164.

67. *Ibid*, p. 166.

68. The two natural gas pipelines will give Russia more flexibility to punish and reward states it perceives in its sphere of influence, particularly in Eastern and Central Europe. This would allow Russia to accurately exploit the susceptibility of many European NATO member states and Ukraine to Russian coercion (as described in Figure 1-4), by depriving them of transit status and effectively isolating them from the West.

69. South Stream will have a similar effect, particularly for countries in the Balkans and South East Europe. However, since South Stream's feasibility is still in question, its potential effects will not be emphasized in this monograph.

70. Lucas, p. 167.

71. Lin, p. 4.

72. This is not the first time that Russia has used its gas pipeline politics to aid in increasing its security; as proven by "Russia's past history of installing fiber optic cable along the Yamal pipeline without informing the Polish government in advance." *Ibid.*

73. Zeyno Baran argues that this project "undermines Europe's efforts to foster the ideals of good governance, market transparency, and democracy both in Russia and in Russia's neighbors." Baran, p. 135.

74. Lucas, p. 166.

75. Marshall Goldman, *Petrostate: Putin, Power, and the New Russia*, New York: Oxford University Press, 2008.

76. Because of this, "RC theory will remain a most important area of study for the immediate and long-term future for Russian and other international groups alike." Thomas, p. 240.

CHAPTER 5

CONCLUSION

Europe risks being caught in an energy stranglehold
by states such as Russia.[1]

Gordon Brown

A 2008 report by the Swedish Defence Research
Agency (FOI) uncovered that Russia has threatened to
disrupt or actually had disrupted natural gas supplies
to countries in its near abroad 40 times since the fall of
the Soviet Union—an account that does not consider
the 2009 Ukraine gas dispute, and several additional
threats to cutoff natural gas supplies to Belarus and
Moldova over the past couple of years.[2] Almost every
time, the use of natural gas as an instrument of unilateral sanctions coincided with political differences
between Russia—the sender—and the target state
(which depended heavily on Russian natural gas).
This monograph emphasizes that with the construction of the Nord Stream and South Stream natural gas
pipelines, and unless alternatives to Russian natural
gas are found, it is only a matter of time until Russia will use natural gas as an instrument of coercion
against NATO member states.

Furthermore, this monograph agrees with Zeyno
Baran's argument that currently "there is still no European strategy to deal with a strong and determined
Russia that uses control of energy supplies, transportation, and distribution to reestablish itself as a major
world power."[3] As Richard Andres explained, "at best,
Europe must live with continuing energy insecurity;
at worst, a total breakdown of negotiations between

127

the supplier and transit country could leave many European countries without heat or electricity."[4] Both options are unacceptable for a continent that houses most members of the North Atlantic Alliance, and member states that are most susceptible to this type of coercion, listed in Figure 2-4, must either address the dependency on Russian natural gas, or brace for the threat of a cold winter at one point over the next decade. Three feasible solutions to the main European vulnerabilities discussed in this monograph require further investigation by academia, industry, and policymakers.

First, the EU must consolidate its bargaining power in its natural gas negotiations vis-à-vis Russia.[5] As underlined in Chapter 4, a divided Europe that does not have a common energy security policy, and a strong instrument to enforce it, is not only a weak Europe, but a household whose members represent a liability for the North Atlantic Alliance.[6] Most countries of Eastern and Central Europe, Europe's periphery, are vulnerable to Russia's use of natural gas as an instrument of coercion, and they are bound to remain so without the support of Europe's center—Germany, France, and Italy. While Russia can afford to disrupt natural gas supplies to individual countries because of the asymmetric interdependence in the trade of natural gas between these states and Russia, as discussed in Chapter 1 and represented in Figure 2-3, Russia cannot and will not use natural gas as an instrument of coercion against a united European front. The consolidation of bargaining power in Europe would underscore that, Russia needs to export its natural gas to Europe as a whole just as much, if not more than, Europe needs to import it from Russia.

Second, while costly to build, bidirectional natural gas pipelines[7] between NATO member states in Europe represent the only way the North Atlantic Alliance can ensure that none of its member states will be bullied by Russia to break with the consensus when grand strategic policies are being considered. Without them, promises by NATO or by Europe's center to protect ECE states, particularly the countries that are members of both NATO and the EU, from Russian coercion will be viewed as empty promises — as indeed such promises have proven to be in the past. Some limited progress has already been made in this field: "[T]wo projects, the Hungary-Romania and Hungary-Croatia interconnectors, were completed before the end of 2010. EEPR [European Energy Programme for Recovery] co-financing is also available for the Romania-Bulgaria and Bulgaria-Greece interconnector projects, making completion highly likely. A Bulgaria-Serbia interconnector also seems likely to materialize."[8]

Lastly, alternatives to Russian natural gas, while expensive, will not only increase NATO and EU energy security, but will also pay off over the long term. The fuels of the distant future in Europe will most likely revolve around renewables, such as solar and wind, and even nuclear power (despite the Fukushima nuclear disaster and Germany's decision to shut all its nuclear reactors by 2022) over the next decades (or until green power will be able to take on the electricity load) Europe will continue to depend "on gas for heating and some electricity, but the bulk of the supply comes from Russia, which hasn't hesitated to use energy as a form of political blackmail."[9] The potentials of liquefied natural gas (LNG)[10] and onshore deposits of shale gas in ECE are huge, and must be considered serious alternatives to Russian natural gas. Access to LNG supplies has already been proven to be a valuable way to increase Europe's supply security as demonstrated during the 2009 Russia–Ukraine gas dispute:

> Accounting for only around 10% of imports of gas in the OECD [The Organization for Economic Co-operation and Development] Europe region in 2008, LNG accounted for 24% of the short-term supply increase that was necessary to compensate for the shortfall in Russian supplies. This confirmed the "swing supply" potential of LNG and its very useful security of supply properties.[11]

Similarly, "natural gas from shale rock promises to provide cleaner, abundant energy"[12] for ECE. However, while experts agree that shale gas "is out there, and it can be accessed,"[13] this monograph also insists that the environmental issues surrounding fracking must be resolved before this alternative is considered.[14]

As it stands now, if Russia "refuses to provide gas or charges an unreasonable price, the consumer cannot quickly or easily turn to another source. The consumer state would have no choice but to accept the supplier's conditions or go without natural gas, an option that is all but unacceptable for most."[15] This creates a situation that undermines the de facto power of NATO in the contemporary security environment, particularly vis-à-vis Russia, unless the dependency on Russian natural gas is promptly addressed.[16]

ENDNOTES - CHAPTER 5

1. Andrei Shleifer and Daniel Treisman, "Why Moscow Says No: A Question of Russian Interests, Not Psychology," *Foreign Affairs*, Vol. 90, No. 1, January 2011, p. 126.

2. Robert L. Larsson, "Energikontroll: Kreml, Gazprom Och Rysk Energipolitik" ("Power Control: The Kremlin, Gazprom, and Russian Energy Policy"), Swedish Defence Research Agency, 2008.

3. Zeyno Baran, "EU Energy Security: Time to End Russian Leverage," *Washington Quarterly*, Vol. 30, No. 4, October, 2007, p. 142.

4. Richard Andres and Michael Kofman, "European Energy Security: Reducing Volatility of Ukraine-Russia Natural Gas Pricing Disputes," *INSS Strategic Forum*, No. 264, February, 2011, p. 1.

5. Edward Christie, Pavel Baev, and Volodymyr Golovko, "Vulnerability and Bargaining Power in EU-Russia Gas Relations," *FIW-Research Reports 2010/11*, No. 3, March, 2011.

6. As was discussed in Chapter 4, and as was further underlined by Zeyno Baran, Director of the Center for Eurasian Policy and a Senior Fellow at the Hudson Institute, who argued that "Russia, the European Union's primary natural gas provider, has deliberately taken advantage of this lack of cohesion to gain favorable energy deals and heighten European dependence on Russian supplies." Baran, p. 131.

7. Robert Cekuta, Interview on the Cost of Natural Gas Infrastructure in Eurasia, March 12, 2011.

8. Christie, Baev, and Golovko.

9. Bryan Walsh, "The Gas Dilemma (Cover Story)," *Time*, Vol. 177, No. 14, April 11, 2011, p. 42.

10. Christophe-Alexandre Paillard, head of the Industrial and Technological Trends Department within the French Ministry of Defense's Strategic Affairs Office, argued that "Europe will have a stronger position vis-à-vis Russia if it develops its liquefied natural gas capacities and diversifies its suppliers. Russia will not be challenged unless Europe refuses to be threatened and blackmailed by threats over energy access. There is still a long way to go and the road is unfortunately paved with many obstacles." Christophe-Alexandre Paillard, "Russia and Europe's Mutual En-

ergy Dependence," *Journal of International Affairs*, Vol. 63, No. 2, Spring 2010, p. 81.

11. Christie, Baev, and Golovko.

12. Walsh, p. 42.

13. Bryan Walsh, the staff writer behind *Time* magazine's Eco-centric blog, argues that "as shale-gas drilling has ramped up, it's been met with a growing environmental backlash. There are complaints about spills and air pollution from closely clustered wells and fears of wastewater contamination from the hydraulic fracturing process--also known as fracking--that is used to tap shale-gas resources." For this reason, Ralph Cavanagh, co-director of the Natural Resources Defense Council's energy program, warns that the shale gas industry "can blow this if it doesn't meet the public's environmental expectations." *Ibid.*, p. 42.

14. The shale gas industry in Europe is doomed to meet with significant legislative challenges in the near future. As discussed earlier in this monograph, the European Union is likely to push forward an agenda against shale gas, due to a wide variety of environmental concerns. France has already banned the further expansion of the shale gas industry. The Chairman of the European Parliament's Environment, Public Health and Food Safety Committee, Jo Leinen, a German Progressive Socialist and an influential Member of the European Parliament, believes Europe needs to look more carefully at shale gas, and at the consequences of pursuing it. As of July 2011, the prospects of shale gas in Europe remain dim at best.

15. Baran, p. 132.

16. Ultimately, this monograph supports Robert Gates's assessment that NATO could face "a dim if not dismal" future, not because of funding considerations but, as discussed in Chapter 4, because NATO decisions are made by consensus. Many members will be unlikely to side against Russia in the future because of their heavy dependency on Russian Natural Gas.

BIBLIOGRAPHY

Aguilera, Roberto F., "The Future of the European Natural Gas Market: A Quantitative Assessment," *Energy*, Vol. 35, No. 8, August 2010, pp. 3332-3339.

Ahrari, Mohammed, "OAPEC and 'Authoritative' Allocation of Oil: An Analysis of the Arab Oil Embargo," *Studies in Comparative International Development*, Vol. 14, No. 1, Spring 1979, p. 9.

Andres, Richard and Michael Kofman, "European Energy Security: Reducing Volatility of Ukraine-Russia Natural Gas Pricing Disputes," *INSS Strategic Forum*, No. 264, February 2011, pp. 1-16.

Apergis, Nicholas and James E. Payne, "Natural Gas Consumption and Economic Growth: A Panel Investigation of 67 Countries," *Applied Energy*, Vol. 87, No. 8, August 2010, pp. 2759-2763.

Arzakanyan, Marina and Tatyana Zvereva, "Three Hundred Years of Cooperation," *International Affairs*, Vol. 57, No. 1, 2011, pp. 12-21.

Askari, Hossein G., John Forrer, Hildy Teegen, and Jiawen Yang, *Economic Sanctions. Examining their Philosophy and Efficacy*, Westport, CT: Praeger, 2003.

Aslund, Anders and Andrew Kuchins, *The Russia Balance Sheet*, Washington, DC: Peterson Institute for International Economics, Center for Strategic and International Studies, 2009.

"Azerbaijan-Romania LNG Project may Cost 4.5bn Euros," *News.Az*, February 15, 2011.

Baldwin, David A., *Economic Statecraft*, Princeton, NJ: Princeton University Press, 1985.

Bapat, Navin A. and T. Clifton Morgan, "Multilateral Versus Unilateral Sanctions Reconsidered: A Test Using New Data," *International Studies Quarterly*, Vol. 53, No. 4, December 2009, pp. 1075–1094.

Baran, ZeyNo. "EU Energy Security: Time to End Russian Leverage," *Washington Quarterly*, Vol. 30, No. 4, October 2007, pp. 131-144.

Barfield, Claude E. and Mark A. Groombridge, "Unilateral Sanctions Undermine U.S. Interests," *The World and I*, December 1, 1998.

Barnes, Joe, Mark H. Hayes, Amy M. Jaffe, and David G. Victor, "Introduction to the Study," in *Natural Gas and Geopolitics from 1970 to 2040*, David G. Victor, Amy M. Jaffe, and Mark H. Hayes, eds., New York: Cambridge University Press, 2006.

Baranovsky, Vladimir, "Russia: A Part of Europe or Apart from Europe?" *International Affairs*, Vol. 76, No. 3, July 2000, p. 443.

Baumann, Florian and Georg Simmerl, *Between Conflict and Convergence: The EU Member States and the Quest for a Common External Energy Policy*, Research Group on European Affairs, 2011.

Belton, Catherine, Neil Buckley, and Roman Olearchyk, "Russia-Ukraine Gas Peace Threatens to Unravel," *Financial Times*, September 23, 2010.

Bhadrakumar, M. K., Amb., "Pipeline Geopolitics: Major Turnaround. Russia, China, Iran Redraw Energy Map. Turkmenistan Commits its Gas Exports to China, Russia & Iran," *Global Research*, January 12, 2010, October 27, 2010. *www.globalresearch.ca/index.php?context=va&aid=16932*.

"Bill Allowing Russia to Run Ukrainian Gas Pipes Coming Soon-Gazprom," *BBC Monitoring Kiev Unit Supplied by BBC Worldwide Monitoring*, September 24, 2010.

Birkner, Christine, "Natural Gas in a Range," *Futures: News, Analysis & Strategies for Futures, Options & Derivatives Traders*, Vol. 39, No. 4, April 2010, p. 16.

Bor, Alexander, "Ukraine Seeks Changes in Terms of Russian Gas Accord," *Platts Oilgram News*, July 5, 2010, p. 7.

Bourdeaux, Richard, "Kremlin Ends Freeze with Kiev, in Relief Over Election," *Wall Street Journal-Eastern Edition*, Vol. 255, No. 20, January 26, 2010, p. A11.

Bozhilova, Diana and Tom Hashimoto, "EU-Russia Energy Negotiations: A Choice between Rational Self-Interest and Collective Action," *European Security*, Vol. 19, No. 4, December 2010, pp. 627-642.

Bremmer, Ian, *The End of the Free Market*, New York: Penguin Group, 2010.

_____. "The Return of State Capitalism." *Survival*, Vol. 50, No. 3, June 2008, pp. 55-64.

Bremmer, Ian and Robert Johnston, "The Rise and Fall of Resource Nationalism," *Survival*, Vol. 51, No. 2, April 2009, pp. 149-158.

Brzezinski, Zbigniew, "An Agenda for NATO," *Foreign Affairs*, Vol. 88, No. 5, September 2009, pp. 2-20.

_____, *Power and Principle: Memoirs of the National Security Adviser, 1977-1981*, New York: Farrar, Straus & Giroux, 1990.

_____, "The Premature Partnership," *Foreign Affairs*, Vol. 73, No. 2, March-April 1994, pp. 67-82.

Cekuta, Robert, *Interview on the Cost of Natural Gas Infrastructure in Eurasia*, Alexander Ghaleb, ed., Interview was based on statements that Robert Cekuta made during his speech at the TISS Energy Security Conference, Raleigh, NC, 2011.

Chan, Steve and Cooper Drury, "Sanctions as Economic Statecraft: An Overview," in *Sanctions as Economic Statecraft*, Steve Chan and Cooper Drury, eds., New York: St. Martin's Press, 2000, pp. 1-16.

Choi, Chong Ju and Diana Digol, "Ethical Infrastructure: A New Requirement of the State's Industrial Policy," *Journal of Public Affairs*, 14723891, Vol. 10, No. 3, August 2010, pp. 225-232.

Christie, Edward, Pavel Baev, and Volodymyr Golovko, "Vulnerability and Bargaining Power in EU-Russia Gas Relations," *FIW-Research Reports 2010/11* No. 3, March 2011.

Cole, Bernard, *Interview on Russia as an Energy Superstate*, Alexander Ghaleb, ed., Interview was based on statements that Dr. Cole made during his speech at the TISS Energy Security Conference, Raleigh, NC, 2011.

Comolli, Virginia, "Energy Security," Chap. 8, in *Europe and Global Security*, Bastian Giegerich, ed., London, UK: International Institute for Strategic Studies, 2010, pp. 177-196.

"Congress Should Do More to Support Natural Gas as Fuel: NGVAmerica Chief," *Bulk Transporter*, Vol. 72, No. 12, June 2010, p. 12.

Country Risk Assessments: Russia and the CIS, Matthew Clements, ed., 24th Ed., Alexandria, VA: Jane's Sentinel, 2009.

Davis, Kathleen, "EU Energy Commissioner Gets on 2020 Bandwagon," *POWERGRID International*, Vol. 15, No. 12, December 2010, pp. 12-14.

de Haas, Marcel, "Medvedev's Security Policy: A Provisional Assessment," *Russian Analytical Digest*, Vol. 62, June 18, 2009, pp. 2-5.

Deutch, John, "The Good News about Gas: The Natural Gas Revolution and its Consequences," *Foreign Affairs*, Vol. 90, No. 1, January 2011, pp. 82-93.

_____," The Natural Gas Revolution," *Wall Street Journal-Eastern Ed.*, Vol. 256, No. 13, July 16, 2010, p. A17.

Devarajan, Shantayanan and Anthony C. Fisher, "Exploration and Scarcity," *The Journal of Political Economy*, Vol. 90, No. 6, December 1982, pp. 1279-1290.

Dimitrakopoulou, Sophia and Andrew Liaropoulos, "Russia's National Security Strategy to 2020: A Great Power in the

Making?" *Caucasian Review of International Affairs*, Vol. 4, No. 1, Winter 2010, pp. 35-42.

Domjan, Paul and Matt Stone, "A Comparative Study of Resource Nationalism in Russia and Kazakhstan 2004-2008," *Europe-Asia Studies*, Vol. 62, No. 1, January 6, 2010, pp. 35-62.

Doran, George, *The Futility of Economic Sanctions as an Instrument of National Power in the 21st Century*, Carlisle, PA: U.S. Army War College, 1998.

Drezner, Daniel, "The Complex Causation of Sanction Outcomes," in *Sanctions as Economic Statecraft*, Steve Chan and Cooper Drury, eds., New York: St. Martin's Press, 2000, pp. 212-233.

_____, *The Sanctions Paradox, Economic Statecraft and International Relations*, New York: Cambridge University Press, 1999.

Eland, Ivan, "Economic Sanctions as Tools of Foreign Policy," in George Lopez and David Cortright, eds., *Economic Sanctions, Panacea Or Peacebuilding in a Post-Cold War World?* Boulder, CO: Westview Press, 1995, pp. 29-42.

Emerson, Michael, *President Yanukovich's Dubious Deal*, Centre for European Policy Studies (CEPS), 2010, *www,ceps,eu/book/president-yanukovich%E2%80%99s-dubious-deal*.

The Energy Strategy of Russia through 2030, Moscow, Russia: Ministry of Energy of the Russian Federation, 2010.

Epperson, Sharon, *Natural Gas is the 'Fuel of the Future': Shell CEO* CNBC.com, 2010.

"Europe Boosts LNG Purchases," *Russia Beyond the Headlines*, June 10, 2010.

Flexibility in Natural Gas Supply and Demand, Paris, France: OECD/IEA, 2002.

Freifeld, Daniel, "The Great Pipeline Opera," *Foreign Policy*, No. 174, September 2009, pp. 120-127.

Galtung, Johan, "On the Effects of International Economic Sanctions: With Examples from the Case of Rhodesia," *World Politics*, Vol. 19, No. 3, April 1967, pp. 378-416.

"Gas Deal Brings Down Yushchenko`s Government," *Current Digest of the Post-Soviet Press*, Vol. 58, No. 1, February 2006, pp. 5-16.

"Gas Poisoning," *Country Monitor*, Vol. 14, No. 2, January 16, 2006, p. 4.

Gas Wars, Vol. 390, Economist Newspaper Limited, 2009.

"Gazprom and Naftogaz Slow to Consolidate," *NEWSBCM*, November 1, 2010, *www,newsbcm,com/doc/397*.

Geropoulos, Costis, "Putin to Ukraine: No Merger, no Gas Talks," *New Europe*, October 31, 2010, *www,neurope,eu/articles/Putin-to-Ukraine-No-merger-no-gas-talks/103481,php*.

Goldman, Marshall, *Petrostate: Putin, Power, and the New Russia*, New York: Oxford University Press, 2008.

Goldman, Minton, ed., *Russia, the Eurasian Republics, and Central/Eastern Europe*, 10th Ed., Dubuque, IO: Global Studies, 2005.

"Government's Gas Counter-Offensive," *Polish News Bulletin*, September 23, 2010.

Gray, Colin, "Inescapable Geography," *Journal of Strategic Studies*, Vol. 22, No. 2, 1999, pp. 161-177.

Greenspan, Alan, Committee on Energy and Commerce, U.S. House of Representatives, *Natural Gas Supply and Demand Issues*, June 10, 2003.

Hawaleshka, Danylo, "The Back-to-Moscow Election?" *Maclean's*, Vol. 123, No. 5, February 15, 2010, pp. 22-23.

Hegburg, Alan, "Keynote Speech on the Impact of Fossil Fuels on Security," Raleigh, NC, Triangle Institute for Security Studies, March 3, 2011.

Hill, Fiona, "Russia: The 21st Century's Energy Superpower?" in *Russia, the Eurasian Republics, and Central/Eastern Europe,* Minton Goldman, ed., 10th Ed., Dubuque, IO: Global Studies, 2005.

Hitler, Adolf, *Private Conversation between Adolf Hitler and the Finnish Military Commander, Marshal Baron Carl Gustav Mannerheim,* Adolf Hitler and Baron Carl Gustav Mannerheim, 1942, Finnish Broadcasting Company, Recording.

Horbach, Volodymyr, "Modern Russia in the Ukrainian Public Sphere," Chap. 3, in *The Perception of Russia in Romania, Republic of Moldova, and Ukraine,* Gabi Radu and Iulian Chifu, eds., Bucharest, Romania: Editura Cartea Veche, 2011, pp. 339-357.

Huber, Peter, "Kill Oil with Natural Gas and Electricity: A Carbon Strategy the World can Afford," *Energy Policy & the Environment Report,* No. 4, September, 2009.

Hufbauer, Gary C., Jeffrey J. Schott, and Kimberly A. Elliott, *Economic Sanctions Reconsidered, History and Current Policy,* 2nd Ed., Washington, DC: Institute for International Economics, 1990.

"INGAA Responds to Report on Reliance of Natural Gas for Electricity," *Underground Construction,* Vol. 65, No. 9, September 2010, p. 8.

Jaffe, Amy M., Mark H. Hayes, and David G. Victor, "Gas Geopolitics: Visions to 2040," Program on Energy and Sustainable Development (PESD), Working Paper #36, Stanford, CA: Institute for International Studies.

Jaffe, Amy M. and Ronald Soligo, "Market Structure in the New Gas Economy: Is Cartelization Possible?" in *Natural Gas and Geopolitics: From 1970 to 2040,* David G. Victor, Amy M. Jaffe, and Mark H. Hayes, eds., New York: Cambridge University Press, 2006.

Kaveshnikov, Nikolay, "The Issue of Energy Security in Relations between Russia and the European Union," *European Security,* Vol. 19, No. 4, December 2010, pp. 585-605.

Kazantsev, Andrey, "The Crisis of GAZPROM as the Crisis of Russia's Energy Super-State Policy Towards Europe and the Former Soviet Union," *Caucasian Review of International Affairs*, Vol. 4, No. 3, Summer 2010, pp. 271-284.

Kelanic, Rosemary, *The Coercive Potential of Oil*, Alexander Ghaleb, ed., Interview conducted after the Energy and Security Initiative Conference, 2011.

_____, "Comments on the Impact of Fossil Fuels on Security," Raleigh, NC: Triangle Institute for Security Studies, March 3, 2011.

Kerr, Richard A. "Natural Gas from Shale Bursts Onto the Scene," *Science*, Vol. 328, No. 5986, June 25, 2010, pp. 1624-1626.

Knott, David, "Black Cloud Over White Night," *Oil & Gas Journal*, November 8, 1993, p. 32.

Kupchinsky, Roman, "LNG-Russia's New Energy Blackmail Tool," *Eurasia Daily Monitor*, Vol. 6, No. 77, April 22, 2009.

Labarre, Frederic, "Russian Neo-Mercantilism," 10th CDAI Graduate Symposium, Kingston, Ontario, Canada, October 26-27, 2007.

Lajtai, Rolan, Annamária Czinkos, and Tamás Dinh, "NABUCCO VS. SOUTH STREAM: The Effects and Feasibility in the Central and Eastern European Region," 24th World Gas Conference, Buenos Aires, Argentina, KPMG in Central and Eastern Europe, October 5-9, 2009.

Larrabee, Stephen F., "Russia, Ukraine, and Central Europe: The Return of Geopolitics," *Journal of International Affairs*, Vol. 63, No. 2, Spring 2010, pp. 33-52.

Larsson, Robert L., "Energikontroll: Kreml, Gazprom Och Rysk Energipolitik," Swedish Defence Research Agency, 2008.

Lefebvre, Vladimir and Victorina Lefebvre, "Reflexive Control: The Soviet Concept of Influencing an Adversary's Decision-making Process," Englewood, CO: SAIC, 1984.

Leonard, Mark and Nicu Popescu, *A Power Audit of EU-Russia Relations*, Cambridge Grove, London: European Council on Foreign Relations, 2007.

Liberman, Peter, "The Spoils of Conquest," *International Security*, Vol. 18, No. 2, Fall 1993, p. 125.

Lin, Christina, *The Prince of Rosh: Russian Energy Imperialism and the Emerging Eurasian Military Alliance of the Shanghai Cooperation Organization*, Berlin, DE: Institute for Strategic-Political-Security-and Economic Consultancy (ISPSW), 2009.

"Lithuania Demands Fair Gas Price from Gazprom," *Reuters*, March 3, 2011.

"Lithuania Demands Fair Price from Gazprom," *The Baltic Times*, March 4, 2011.

Lopez, George and David Cortright, "Assessing Smart Sanctions: Lessons from the 1990s," in *Smart Sanctions: Targeting Economic Statecraft*, George Lopez and David Cortright, eds., Lanham, MD: Rowman & Littlefield Publishers, Inc., 2002.

Lucas, Edward, *The New Cold War: Putin's Russia and the Threat to the West*, New York: Palgrave MacMillan, 2009.

Lugar, Dick, "Senator Lugar's Keynote Speech to the German Marshall Fund Conference in Advance of the NATO Summit," Riga, Latvia, November 27, 2006.

_____, "Speech to the U.S.- Ukraine Energy Dialogue Series," Washington, DC, April 15, 2008.

Mackinder, H. J., "The Geographical Pivot of History," *The Geographical Journal*, Vol. 23, No. 4, April 1904, pp. 421-437.

Mahnovski, Sergej, "Natural Resources and Potential Conflict in the Caspian Sea Region," Chap. 5, in *Fault-Lines of Conflict in Central Asia and the South Caucasus*, Thomas Szayna, ed., Santa Monica, CA: RAND, 2003.

Maital, Shlomo, "What We Can Offer Russia," *The Jerusalem Report*, October 22, 1992, p. 56.

Mankoff, Jeffrey, *Eurasian Energy Security*: Council on Foreign Relations, 2009.

Mansfield, Edward D., "Alliances, Preferential Trading Arrangements and Sanctions," *Journal of International Affairs*, Vol. 48, No. 1, Summer 1994, p. 119.

Mansourov, Alexandre, "Mercantilism and Neo-Imperialism in Russian Foreign Policy during President Putin's 2nd Term," *The Korean Journal of Defense Analysis*, Vol. 17, No. 1, Spring 2005, pp. 151-184.

Márquez, Carlos and Gina M, Hernández, "Everybody is on Board: Increased Use of Natural Gas Essential to Reduce Energy Costs in the Short Term," *Caribbean Business*, Vol. 38, No. 15, April 22, 2010, pp. 20-27.

_____, "Natural Gas: The Cleanest Fossil Fuel Catches on," *Caribbean Business*, Vol. 38, No. 15, April 22, 2010, p. 27.

Maxwell, Don and Zhen Zhu, "Natural Gas Prices, LNG Transport Costs, and the Dynamics of LNG Import," *Energy Economics*, Vol. 33, No. 2, March 2011, pp. 217-226.

Mearsheimer, John J., "The Case for a Ukrainian Nuclear Deterrent," *Foreign Affairs*, Vol. 72, No. 3, Summer 1993, pp. 50-66.

Medvedev, Alexander, "The Economic Crisis and the Future of the Gas Sector," *International Affairs*, Vol. 57, No. 1, 2011, pp. 188-191.

Mitrany, David, *The Problem of International Sanctions*, London, UK: Oxford University Press, 1925.

Morgan, T. Clifton, Navin Bapat, and Valentin Krustev, "The Threat and Imposition of Economic Sanctions, 1971-2000," *Conflict Management and Peace Science*, Vol. 26, No. 1, February, 2009, pp. 92-110.

Morozov, Viatcheslav, "Imperial Discourse in Russian International Studies: Empire vs. the Corporatist State as Images of

Putin's Russia," 4th CEEISA Convention, University of Tartu, Estonia, June 26, 2006.

"Natural Gas' Path to Low-Carbon Future," *USA Today Magazine*, Vol. 139, No. 2782, July 2010, p. 7-7.

"Natural Gas Fueling Station Locations," Department of Energy, *www,afdc,energy,gov/afdc/fuels/natural_gas_locations,html*.

Newell, Richard, "Annual Energy Outlook 2011: Reference Case," Washington, DC: The Paul H, Nitze School of Advanced International Studies, December 16, 2010.

Newnham, Randall E., "More Flies with Honey: Positive Economic Linkage in German Ostpolitik from Bismarck to Kohl," *International Studies Quarterly*, Vol. 44, No. 1, March 2000, pp. 73.

Ngobi, James, "The United Nations Experience with Sanctions," in *Economic Sanctions: Panacea Or Peacebuilding in a Post-Cold War World*? George Lopez and David Cortright, eds., Boulder, CO: Westview Press, 1995, pp. 17-27.

Nurnberger, Ralph, "Why Sanctions (almost) Never Work," *The International Economy*, Vol. 17, No. 4, Fall 2003, pp. 71-72.

Oganesyan, Armen, "Energy Industry and Ecology," *International Affairs*, Vol. 57, No. 1, 2011, pp. 216-230.

Opening Address to the Security Council Meeting on the Issue of Russia's Role in Guaranteeing International Energy Security, December 26, 2005.

"Opinion Poll: Nationalism in Contemporary Russia," *Russian Analytical Digest*, Vol. 93, March 10, 2011, pp. 10-11.

Orbán, Anita, *Power, Energy, and the New Russian Imperialism*, Westport, CT: Praeger Security International, 2008.

Paillard, Christophe-Alexandre, "Russia and Europe's Mutual Energy Dependence," *Journal of International Affairs*, Vol. 63, No. 2, Spring 2010, pp. 65-84.

Pavlov, Nikolai, "Twenty Years of German Unity," *International Affairs*, Vol. 57, No. 1, 2011, pp. 72-84.

Perepelytsya, Hrygoriy, "Russia in State Policies of Ukraine," Chap. 3, in *The Perception of Russia in Romania, Republic of Moldova, and Ukraine*, Gabi Radu and Iulian Chifu, eds., Bucharest, Romania: Editura Cartea Veche, 2011, pp. 358-375.

Petrovsky, Pavel and Vladimir Dedushkin, "Quo Vadis, NATO? A Glance from Lisbon," *International Affairs*, Vol. 57, No. 1, 2011, pp. 49-57.

Press-Barnathan, Galia, *Economic Cooperation and the Transition Away from Conflictual Relations: The Neglected Side of Commercial Liberalism*, 2004.

Putin, Vladimir Vladimirovich, "The Strategic Planning of Regional Natural Resources Under the Formation of Market Relations," Thesis for Ph.D. in Economics, Saint Petersburg State Mining University, 1997.

"Putin's Gas Squeeze," *Wall Street Journal-Eastern Ed.*, Vol. 247, No. 1, January 3, 2006, pp. A24.

Raiklin, Ernest, *After Gorbachev? A Mechanism for the Transformation of Totalitarian State Capitalism into Authoritarian Mixed Capitalism*, Issue 20 of *Journal of Social, Political, and Economic Studies* Monograph Series, Washington, DC: Council for Social and Economic Studies, 1989.

"The Regulatory Effects of Russia and Ukraine's 'Gas War' are Emerging," *MarketWatch: Global Round-Up*, Vol. 8, No. 9, September 2009, pp. 171-172.

Riabchuk, Mykola, "Ukraine's Nuclear Nostalgia," *World Policy Journal*, Vol. 26, No. 4, Winter 2009, pp. 95-105.

"Russia and France: A New Quality of Relations," *International Affairs*, Vol. 57, No. 1, 2011, pp. 22-43.

"Russia/Ukraine: Putin's Gas-Merger Plan," *Business Eastern Europe*, Vol. 39, No. 16, May 3, 2010, pp. 1-2.

"Russia: Ukrainian Natural Gas Purchases Cut," *STRATFOR*, September 30, 2010.

Rutland, Peter, "Russia as an Energy Superpower," *New Political Economy*, Vol. 13, No. 2, June 2008, pp. 203-210.

Sandalow, David, "Keynote Speech to Battery Technology for Transportation: From Scientific Discovery to Marketplace Event," Washington, DC: The Brookings Institution, February 8, 2011.

Schecter, Jerrold, *Russian Negotiating Behavior,* Washington, DC: United States Institute of Peace Press, 1998.

Shaffer, Edward Harry, "Canada's Oil and Imperialism," *International Journal of Political Economy*, Vol. 35, No. 2, Summer 2006, pp. 54-71.

Shleifer, Andrei and Daniel Treisman, "Why Moscow Says No: A Question of Russian Interests, Not Psychology," *Foreign Affairs*, Vol. 90, No. 1, January 2011, pp. 122-138.

Smith, Keith, *Russia-Europe Energy Relations, Implications for U.S. Policy,* Washington DC: CSIS, 2010.

Sopinska, Joanna, "Eu/Ukraine : Yanukovych Wins Praise for Energy Sector Reforms," *Europolitics Daily in English)*, September 15, 2010.

Sperandei, Maria, "Between Rational Choice and Historical Contingency: The Hidden Dilemma of Multiple Objectives in the Study of Economic Sanctions," *Conference Papers-International Studies Association*, 2009, pp. 1-34.

Stern, Roger, "Oil Market Power and United States National Security," *Proceedings of the National Academy of Sciences of the United States of America*, Vol. 103, No. 5, January 31, 2006, pp. 1650-1655.

Stevens, Paul, "National Oil Companies and International Oil Companies in the Middle East: Under the Shadow of Government and the Resource Nationalism Cycle," *Journal of World Energy Law & Business*, Vol. 12, No. 1, 2008, pp. 5-30.

Stepanenko, Svetlana, "Ukrainian Foreign Minister Deplores Russian 'Blackmail' Over Gas Prices; Some in Ukraine Want to Invoke International Guarantees of its Security Pledged in 1994 When it Gave Up Nuclear Arms; Russian Navy Chief: Terms of Black Sea Fleet Basing," *Current Digest of the Post-Soviet Press*, Vol. 57, No. 51, January 18, 2006, pp. 7-8.

"A Storm is Brewing in the East Despite Temporary Gas Truce," *MarketWatch: Energy*, Vol. 5, No. 8, August 2006, pp. 19-21.

Sushko, Oleksan, Dr. "Russian Economic Presence in Ukraine: Interests Evolution and Current Trends," Chap. 3, in *The Perception of Russia in Romania, Republic of Moldova, and Ukraine*, Gabi Radu and Iulian Chifu, eds., Bucharest, Romania: Editura Cartea Veche, 2011, pp. 329-338.

"Swinoujscie LNG Gas Terminal, Baltic Coast, Poland," *Hydrocarbons Technology*, *www,hydrocarbons-technology,com/projects/swinoujscie/*.

Taylor, Brendan, *Sanctions as Grand Strategy*, New York: The International Institute for Strategic Studies, 2010.

Thomas, Timothy L., "Russia's Reflexive Control Theory and the Military," *Journal of Slavic Military Studies*, Vol. 17, No. 2, April 2004, pp. 237-256.

Thompson, Wayne, *Nordic, Central, and Southeastern Europe*, 5th Ed., Harpers Ferry, WV: Stryker-Post Publications, 2005.

Thorpe, Keir, "The Forgotten Shortage: Britain's Handling of the 1967 Oil Embargo," *Contemporary British History*, Vol. 21, No. 2, June 2007, pp. 201-222.

Thorun, Christian, *Explaining Change in Russian Foreign Policy: The Role of Ideas in Post-Soviet Russia's Conduct Towards the West*, New York: Palgrave MacMillan, 2009.

Tsygankov, Andrei, "Russia's Foreign Policy," Chap. 10, in *After Putin's Russia: Past Imperfect, Future Uncertain,* Stephen K. Wegren and Dale R. Herspring, 4th Ed., Plymouth, UK: Rowman & Littlefield Publishers, Inc., 2010, pp. 223-242.

Tsygankov, Andrei P. and Pavel A. Tsygankov, "National Ideology and IR Theory: Three Incarnations of the 'Russian Idea'," *European Journal of International Relations,* Vol. 16, No. 4, December 2010, pp. 663-686.

Tubb, Rita, *Future Role of Natural Gas and Shale Revolution Dominate at P&GJ's 2010 Pipeline Opportunities Conference,* Vol. 237, Oildom Publishing Company of Texas, Inc., 2010.

_____, "Study Finds Nation's Natural Gas Supply Will Last Well into Next Century," *Pipeline & Gas Journal,* Vol. 237, No. 4, April 2010, pp. 34-36.

"Ukraine Suspends Gas Supply to Poland at Russia's Request," *BBC Monitoring Kiev Unit Supplied by BBC Worldwide Monitoring,* September 27, 2010.

"Ukraine Wants Naftogaz and Gazprom Joint Venture Soon Says PM," *RIA Novosti-Kiev,* April 12, 2011.

Ullman, Richard H., "Redefining Security," *The MIT Press, International Security,* Vol. 8, No. 1, Summer 1983, pp. 129-153.

"Uneven Prospects for Natural-Gas Vehicles," *Machine Design,* Vol. 82, No. 13, August 12, 2010, pp. 23-26.

United Nations Security Council Resolution, Public Law 1973, 2011.

Urban, Julie A., "US Access to the Global LNG Market," *OPEC Energy Review,* Vol. 32, No. 3, September 2008, pp. 215-231.

Vavra, Bob, "1973: The Arab Oil Embargo Transforms the World," *National Petroleum News,* Vol. 92, No. 12, November, 2000, pp. 18.

Victor, David G, "What Resource Wars?" *National Interest,* No. 92, November 2007, pp. 48-55.

Victor, Nadejda and David G. Victor, "Bypassing Ukraine: Exporting Russian Gas to Poland and Germany," in *Natural Gas and Geopolitics, from 1970 to 2040,* David G. Victor, Amy M. Jaffe, and Mark H. Hayes, eds., New York: Cambridge University Press, 2006.

Wagman, David, "Natural Gas Rising," *Power Engineering,* Vol. 114, No. 10, October 2010, p. 6.

Wald, Matthew L., "Study Says Natural Gas use Likely to Double," *New York Times,* June 25, 2010, p. 3.

Walsh, Bryan, "The Gas Dilemma (Cover Story)," *Time,* Vol. 177, No. 14, April 11, 2011, pp. 40-48.

Wegren, Stephen K. and Dale R. Herspring, eds., *After Putin's Russia: Past Imperfect, Future Uncertain,* 4th Ed., Plymouth, UK: Rowman & Littlefield Publishers, Inc., 2010.

Williams, James C., *The History of Energy, Scientists and the Franklin Institute Making their Cases,* Philadelphia, PA: The Franklin Institute, 2006.

"The Winter Gas War," *Wall Street Journal-Eastern Edition,* Vol. 253, No. 5, January 7, 2009, p. A12.

Zeihan, Peter, "Ukraine's Election and the Russian Resurgence," *STRATFOR,* January 26, 2010.

U.S. ARMY WAR COLLEGE

Major General Gregg F. Martin
Commandant

*****

STRATEGIC STUDIES INSTITUTE

Director
Professor Douglas C. Lovelace, Jr.

Director of Research
Dr. Antulio J. Echevarria II

Author
Captain Alexander Ghaleb

Director of Publications
Dr. James G. Pierce

Publications Assistant
Ms. Rita A. Rummel

*****

Composition
Mrs. Jennifer E. Nevil

www.ingramcontent.com/pod-product-compliance
Lightning Source LLC
Chambersburg PA
CBHW080017280326
41934CB00015B/3378

9 781780 399850